Top Notch Executive Interviews

Top Notch Executive Interviews

How to Strategically Deal With Recruiters,
Search Firms, Boards of Directors, Panels,
Presentations, Pre-interviews, and Other
High-Stress Situations

By Katharine Hansen, PhD

CAREER
PRESS

Franklin Lakes, NJ

TOP NOTCH EXECUTIVE INTERVIEWS
EDITED BY KATE HENCHES
TYPESET BY DIANA GHAZZAWI
Cover design by Rob Johnson/Johnson Design
Printed in the U.S.A. by Courier

To order this title, please call toll-free 1-800-CAREER-1 (NJ and Canada: 201-848-0310) to order using VISA or MasterCard, or for further information on books from Career Press.

CAREER
PRESS

The Career Press, Inc., 3 Tice Road, PO Box 687,
Franklin Lakes, NJ 07417
www.careerpress.com

Library of Congress Cataloging-in-Publication Data
Hansen, Katharine.
   Executive interviews : how to strategically deal with recruiters, search firms,
   boards of directors, panels, presentations, pre-interviews, and other high-stress
   situations / by Katharine Hansen.
        p. cm.
   Includes index.
   ISBN 978-1-60163-084-1
      1. Employment interviewing. 2. Executives--Employment. 3. Executives--
   Recruiting. I. Title.

HF5549.5.I6H345 2010
650.14'4--dc22
                                                           2009034269

Dedicated to Randall S. Hansen, PhD.

Your love, support, advice, editorial suggestions, and contributions were immeasurable and invaluable. Most importantly, I will always associate this book with our first ecstatic weeks at EmpoweringRetreat and how you made it all possible.

Contents

Introduction:
The Executive
Interview Difference

At no time in recent history have executive career paths been as likely to change as they have since the global economic crisis unfolded dramatically in 2008. At no time have executives experienced a greater need to reinvent themselves. The *2009 Executive Job Market Intelligence Report* by ExecuNet revealed that executives were caught by surprise by the displacements the crisis sparked and that the vast majority of those surveyed were considering changing industries. [downloadable from *http://www.execunet.com/executive-jobs-report.cfm*]. Thus, at no time has the executive employment interview presented a greater challenge.

Executive interviews have always been fraught with challenges—because they are different from interviews for candidates at lower levels.

In the executive-interview process, for example:

- o Candidates often undergo a longer interview cycle with more and longer interviews than for lower-level positions. For the first interview alone "it is common for executive candidates to have a full day of interviewing in which they meet with various interviewers," notes executive career coach Cheryl Palmer of CalltoCareer.com, and the day-long process includes lunch, during which time the interviewee is still being interviewed. Furthermore, the interview process can drag on for a long time.

o Executives need to prove they're "A Players." For their top professional slots, employers seek "someone who can not just meet the demands of their original mandate," says Tom Adam, a Los Angeles-based senior contract recruiter, "but take the next step and bring about novel and productive solutions to either address previously unrecognized needs, take the company to that next level of success—*that*'s the person you hope to find." Employers want to hire candidates with passion and initiative who can motivate others and inspire productivity while embracing new ideas.

o Executives need a comprehensive grasp on the prospective employer's needs and challenges—as well as a vision to meet the needs and tackle the challenges. Candidates at every level are expected to do their homework—to have thoroughly researched the prospective employer before an interview. But at the executive level, the research must dig deeply into the needs, challenges, and issues the employer faces. Candidates must then demonstrate the capacity to offer ideas and solutions to meet the needs and challenges. But they must tread a fine line and not suggest solutions that have already been tried or that are inappropriate for the targeted organization. Instead, they must ask the right questions, as well as discuss similar problems they've solved for past employers.

o A clearly articulated vision for the future of the company or subordinate entity (division, department) the executive will helm is expected. Especially at the highest levels, candidates must be savvy about the prospective employer's growth opportunities and the threats to those opportunities. They must envision how to effectively lead and motivate employees to foster the growth and beat back the threats. New attention to cost-cutting and efficiencies will be required. The candidate must know how to innovate and initiate. On top of all these requirements, the prospective leader must clearly express a vision that turns strategy into execution.

o More than candidates at other levels, executives may be expected to participate in presentations, simulations, problem-solving, and hands-on assignments. At the executive level, mere interviewing often will not be enough. Candidates may be asked to participate in activities such as conducting in-basket exercises, providing 30/60/90-day plans for the targeted employer, and delivering presentations.

o Executive-interview questions may be deeper and more thought-provoking than those for lower-level positions. While the traditional queries found on countless lists of frequently asked interview questions are still used in executive interviews, especially phone interviews and other screening sessions early in the process, most questions will be complex and often behavior-based as the process progresses. Interviewers will probe past professional behaviors that predict the kinds of results employers can expect the candidate to contribute.

o Interviewees may be asked to elaborate and dig deeper with their responses. Interviewers will frequently be unsatisfied with even the most eloquent response to a question. Probing follow-up questions that begin "Tell me more about..." are common at this level. Candidates must be ready.

o Executives are expected to have a clear vision of their career paths (for example, a five-year plan) even in the face of a climate in which once-steady career paths are now uncertain. Interviewers want to know how executives see their career plans over the next five to ten years. In part, they want to ensure that the opportunity they're offering aligns with the candidate's planned path. This type of career forecasting has become much more difficult for professionals as a result of an uncertain economy. In the July 2009 issue of the *Journal of Corporate Recruiting Leadership*,

Michael Kannisto predicted "the traditional career path and all its assumptions...will be gone." [http://www.crljournal.com/ exact reference to come upon publication of this issue; statement previewed in article here: http://www.ere.net/2009/05/28/ the-traditional-career-path-will-disappear/] Candidates will thus need to adjust their projected paths for a changing landscape.

o Executives are expected to frame their accomplishments in measurable terms. "Senior executives need to include accomplishments around gross and net profits, revenues, shareholder value, board and investor relations, organic and acquisition growth strategies, capitalization, industry position ranking, new business development, strategic alliances and partnerships, mergers, restructurings, reorganizations, vision and mission, and leading and motivating teams to champion that mission and vision," states executive career coach Beverly Harvey of HarveyCareers.com. They also must present metrics that demonstrate success in quantitative terms. The qualitative human factors are important, too. "I look for a track record of relevant successes and whether or not they give credit to others for that success," says Bill Ward, principal at GMR Executive Search in Arcadia, Calif. "That's typically one of the traits you'll find in an effective leader." Expert career and human resource consultant Sharon McCormick of Durham, N.C., points out that interviewers need to know "how well the candidate can act as an agent of change, demonstrating creativity, flexibility, and innovation" and seek "examples that demonstrate resilience in championing one's vision for the organization to all staff, and how successful the candidate is in leading people through these changes."

o Hiring managers place a high value on executive image. In an executive interview, "image is critically important," says Robyn Feldberg, president of Abundant Success Career Services in Frisco, Tex. Image, Feldberg notes, covers the way the executive carries himself or herself, attire, grooming, connecting skills, and self-expression that is clear, concise, and powerful. Employers want candidates who project a leadership image.

- The executive candidate may be evaluated on the prospective relationship with the company's board of directors. Executives "are often apt to report to a board rather than one boss," points out Barb Poole, president of Hire Imaging, LLC, in St. Cloud, Minn. "When interviewing for a C-level position, you have to consider that your prospective bosses, the board of directors, will want to know how you are going to establish a healthy relationship with them," Poole says. Working with her clients, Poole cites Carly Fiorina, formerly of Hewlett-Packard, "who clearly did not establish that relationship and was fired in a very public arena."

- Interviewers and interviewees function at a higher intensity level. "Executive interviews are more intense because there is more at stake," Palmer notes. Because of the cost incurred in replacing an executive, "hiring managers are very cautious," Palmer says.

- Hiring managers ask questions that probe specific executive competencies. McCormick points to more than two dozen executive competencies that can be addressed in a senior-level interview. Chief among those competencies, says ExecuNet's *Executive Job Market Intelligence Report*, is "identifying the skills the company needs to solve problems and create organizational efficiency." A rapidly emerging competency is cost-cutting, the report states [downloadable from *http://www.execunet. com/executive-jobs-report.cfm*].

  "Hiring managers and human-resources professionals require very precise information from candidates about these executive-level competencies," McCormick says. "Interviewers," she notes, will probe "the scope and depth of the candidate's ability to lead long-term changes as aligned with an organization's mission and balanced with short-term operational steps taken to achieve those goals."

- Executives are subject to more careful vetting. Background checks for high-level candidates are increasingly common and often staggeringly rigorous. Candidates need to know how to avoid land mines in this process.

If the next step in your career is an executive, senior-level, or C-level position, this book will show you how to interview effectively for a position such as Chief Executive Officer, Chief Financial Officer, Chief Information Officer, Chief Marketing Officer, Chief Operations Officer, Customer Service Manager, Director of Operations, Director of Sales, District Manager, Division Manager/Director, Executive Director, Executive Sales Manager, Executive VP, First VP, General Manager, Human Resources Director, Information Systems Director, Logistics Manager, MIS Director, National Sales Manager, Operations Manager, President, Production Manager, Regional Manager, Second VP, Security Director, Senior VP, Telecommunications Director, VP of Business Development, VP of Finance, VP of Manufacturing, VP of Marketing, VP of Operations, or VP of Production.

Here's how this book can assist you in preparing to meet the high expectations decision-makers have of executives in interviews:

Chapter 1 acknowledges that to succeed in interviews, executives must first be invited for interviews and provides a brief overview of landing interviews through personal branding, networking, working with recruiters, crafting an executive resume and cover letter, and following up after you've contacted the employer or recruiter.

In Chapter 2, you'll learn how to conduct the crucial research that will prepare you for every interview aspect.

Chapter 3 guides you through your interview image and the nonverbal aspects of your interview preparation—from your handshake to facial expressions to the way you sit in the chair.

In Chapter 4, you'll learn key characteristics of the many executive-interview formats and content types and how to prepare them.

Chapter 5 introduces you to the kinds of questions to expect and sample responses that have helped executives succeed in top-level interviews. The chapter also helps you to analyze each question to understand what the interviewer's motivation is in asking it and choose the best strategy for responding.

Chapter 6 covers tricky and sticky situations and explains how to keep them from derailing your executive interview—from building rapport in the interview, to handling a poor interviewer, to explaining your reasons for leaving a current job.

Chapter 7 guides you through vital post-interview steps—thank-yous, follow-ups, references, vetting, and background checks. The chapter also guides you in conducting an instructive "post-mortem" to analyze your performance after the interview.

Chapter 8 provides an overview of how to evaluate and negotiate your job offer and compensation package, as well as how to choose from among multiple offers.

In the Appendices, you'll find comprehensive resources, including books, Websites, and a listing of executive interview coaches, to guide you in your interviewing endeavors.

①

A Crash Course in Landing the Interview

Before you can succeed in an interview, you must land the interview. Many books (including this book's companion volume, *Top Notch Executive Resumes*) and resources cover the steps to landing an interview in great detail. (See Appendix B for resources in areas in which you need to freshen your knowledge.) This chapter provides an overview of the seven most important aspects of each of these key elements that lead to obtaining interviews:

1. Building a personal brand
2. Targeting employers
3. Networking
4. Working with recruiters
5. Preparing an effective resume
6. Writing a stellar cover letter
7. Following up on your initial application

Building a personal brand

1. The starting point in your job search should be defining your personal brand—who you are, your promise of value, and why you should be sought out. It should encapsulate your reputation and describe the added value you bring to the employment situation in which you want to see yourself.

2. Your brand should convey your distinctiveness, passion, and unique understanding of the business environment. It must answer the employer's question: Why you over any other candidate? What sets you apart from others?

3. Create a distinctive appearance for all your career-marketing communications that conveys your brand (or enlist a professional to help you create this look). Your resume, cover letter, business cards, thank-you letters, portfolio, personal Website, and more, should package you with a consistent, branded look. Every time an employer sees this look, he or she will instantly associate it with you.

4. Your branding effort should include your online presence. Google yourself to see that plenty of positive information pops up about you (because employers will do the same). If you don't have a strong online presence, create one with a compelling profile on the professional networking site LinkedIn. Consider establishing your own Website with your name as its domain name (such as mine, *katharinehansenphd.com*). You could include a portfolio of your best work or a blog—or both—on the site. Also consider writing articles for other sites and online media outlets showcasing your expertise.

5. Strive to eliminate any negative information online that damages your brand. Remove any controversial material (such as information that reveals religious or political affiliation) or photos you can control. Politely ask site owners to remove negative material on sites you can't control. Counteract negative information you can't eliminate by ensuring plenty of recent positive information.

Targeting employers

1. Your job search will be much more effective if you target the specific employers you want to work for. Marketers, as you know, have increasingly moved away from disseminating advertising messages to mass audiences. So must you avoid sending out hundreds of resumes or posting your resume on dozens of job boards. Only about 1 percent of executives surveyed found career options by widely broadcasting their resumes, as reported in ExecuNet's *2009 Executive Job Market Intelligence Report*. [downloadable from *http://www.execunet.com/executive-jobs-report.cfm*] "The overwhelming majority of positions with an annual salary of $200,000+ are not posted on the wide open web," reported Robyn Greenspan, editor of ExecuNet's newsletter, *Executive Insider*. Focus your efforts on the employers who are the best fit for your talents and who you will most enjoy working for.

2. Identify a list of about 20 employers to target and, using the resources in Chapter 2, conduct extensive research so you know the best ways to target these organizations. Your research should also help you identify hiring managers for the types of positions that interest you.

3. Use your research and your network (see next section) to identify company insiders who can share information and refer you to hiring managers.

4. Consider conducting informational interviews with insiders to learn information you can't find with your other research—about needs, problems, issues, and upcoming initiatives that will enable you to present yourself as the solution to the organization's challenges and leader of its innovations. See the Informational Interviewing Tutorial at *www.quintcareers.cominformational_interviewing.html* to learn more about informational interviews.

5. Integrate your findings on targeted employers into a multifaceted campaign that includes direct mail, networking, responding to job postings from the targeted employers, and when possible, seeking out recruiters who represent any of the targeted organizations.

Networking

1. Especially at the executive level, far more professionals—73 percent according to ExecuNet's *2009 Executive Job Market Intelligence Report*—obtain jobs through networking than any other way. [downloadable from *http://www.execunet.com/executive-jobs-report.cfm*] Thus, networking should be a major component of your job search.

2. One of the best networking venues for executives is professional organizations and associations. Join organizations in your field, attend meetings and events, and network with members.

3. As the linchpin of your networking efforts, ask for advice and referrals; don't ask network contacts for a job. Always thank your contacts for even the smallest effort on your behalf.

4. Don't wait until you need a job to build and connect with your network. Contact members of your network regularly. Offer your help to those who are struggling with economy-provoked job displacement. Be a mentor to those who can learn from you.

5. Online professional networking and social-media sites such as LinkedIn and Facebook are increasingly seen as crucial networking tools. Enhance your networking efforts with these tools, but don't wile away hours online at the expense of far more effective face-to-face networking.

Working with recruiters

1. At the senior and executive levels, recruiters and executive-search firms will be more important to you than they are to job-seekers at lower levels. You may find yourself sought out or "headhunted." Recruiters and search consultants will always be more interested in you if you are employed. As unfair as it may seem, unemployed candidates carry a slight taint of "damaged goods."

2. The recruiter represents the client employer, not the candidate. Thus, he or she does not work for you and is not in business to find you a job. Some recruiters prefer to keep a "supply" of

appropriate candidates in their database to draw from when a matching search assignment comes up. Others will be receptive to contact from you only when they are working on a matching search. Learn the preferred operational style of any recruiter you are considering approaching.

3. Identify the recruiters that specialize in your criteria, such as your field, job function, geographic region, and targeted employers (although you may have difficulty identifying client employers as this information is often confidential).

4. Send your resume and cover letter to a handful of the recruiters you've identified and ask to be considered for appropriate search assignments. Be sure to follow any instructions on resume submission you find on the recruiters' Websites or through calling the support staff. Follow up with a phone call or two (or perhaps a phone call and an e-mail) to request a meeting with the recruiter, but don't make a pest of yourself. The recruiter may meet with you with the idea of keeping you in mind for future searches or may do so only if you fit an active search. Once you begin working with a recruiter, expect coaching for your interview process with the client employer, debriefing after the interview, and guidance in negotiating your compensation package should you get the offer.

5. A terrific way to endear yourself to a recruiter who does not currently have a search assignment that fits your credentials is to refer matching candidates to the recruiter. The recruiter will likely be grateful and remember you when an appropriate assignment comes up.

Preparing an effective resume

1. Your resume must target your desired career goal with precision. An employer taking a quick glance should be able to immediately grasp the job you're targeting, the need you will fill, and the value you can contribute. The executive resume must focus on key strengths that position you to meet a specific need and target specific jobs/employers. A one-size-fits-all resume is

especially ineffective at the executive level. Hiring decision-makers expect your resume to be precisely tailored to the position you're applying for. The reader should never have to guess or wade through copious text to determine what job you want and what you'd be good at.

2. The executive resume must—with a future-oriented flavor—emphasize results, outcomes, and career-defining performance indicators. Using numbers, context, and meaningful metrics, the resume must paint a picture of the executive in action—meeting needs/challenges, solving problems, impacting the company's big picture, growing the business, enhancing revenue, and driving profits. Concrete, measurable accomplishments are the points that sell you.

3. Today's executive resume builds on the executive brand you've developed and communicates the brand's relevance to targeted employers. The branding expressed in your resume captures your career identity, authenticity, passion, essence, and image. Weave your branded message throughout your resume; ensure your branding remains consistent and does not contradict the image you want to project. Branding in the executive resume must include a uniqueness factor that takes your resume to the next level by portraying you as not only *in* the position, but the best person for the position, even the only logical choice for the position. When you imbue your resume with your uniqueness, you show that you completely comprehend the challenges the organization faces and that you are overwhelmingly qualified to meet those challenges. If you have adequately sold your uniqueness, the reader reviewing your resume should say, "This candidate gets it."

4. Ensure that your resume contains relevant keywords. The vast majority of resumes submitted to employers today are handled by applicant tracking systems. Because applicant tracking software and keyword-searchable databases dominate today's hiring process, successful executive resumes must feature keywords based on cutting-edge industry jargon.

5. Consider having your resume professionally written and designed. At the executive level, a resume crafted by a trained professional is a wise investment. Many of the executive interview coaches listed in Appendix B also write resumes.

Writing a stellar cover letter

1. Don't send your resume without a cover letter. Not all hiring decision-makers read them, but because you don't know which ones don't, it's best to err on the side of including a cover letter rather than omitting it. Your sharply focused resume will instantly tell the reader your job target, but with a cover letter, you can expand on the type of position you seek and describe in detail exactly how you qualify for that position. A cover letter can also highlight aspects of your background that are most useful to the prospective employer. Your letter can explain in a positive way circumstances that your resume probably doesn't—such as gaps in your employment history, relocation, and reentry into the job market after a period of entrepreneurship, or a career change. You can emphasize in a cover letter your willingness to travel or relocate. A cover letter is also a window into your personality. A good cover letter can suggest to an employer, "I'd like to interview this person; she sounds like someone I'd like to get to know better. This go-getter seems like just the kind of dynamic executive this organization needs."

2. Send an original letter to each employer. Given that a major function of the cover letter is to go beyond the resume in tailoring your qualifications to specific jobs, a boilerplate cover letter sent to multiple employers is pointless. That's not to say your letter can't have some boilerplate elements; just be sure to customize the bulk of the letter to each recipient.

3. Address the letter to a named individual, ideally the hiring manager. The research resources in Chapter 2 can help you find this person's name if it's not included in the job posting. Avoid writing to the human resources department if possible—or write to

both the HR department and the hiring manager. Avoid such salutations as "Dear Sir or Madam," "Dear Human Resources Director," or "To Whom it May Concern."

4. Steer clear of simply rehashing/highlighting your resume. Draw the reader in with a compelling, interesting letter. Eschew long, boring sentences and paragraphs. Use simple language and uncomplicated sentence structure. Ruthlessly eliminate all unnecessary words. Banish typos, misspellings, and grammatical errors. Stick to one page. Remember that your cover letter as serves as a sample of your communication skills.

5. Take a proactive approach with your last paragraph. State how you plan to follow up the letter (usually with a phone call). Be sure to give a time frame—and then be sure to do what you said you would do.

Following up on your initial application

1. Any time you send out your resume and cover letter—whether in response to an ad or job posting, as part of a direct-mail campaign, or as part of an effort to reach recruiters—follow up shortly afterwards—a week to 10 days.

2. You will often read the phrase "No phone calls" in job postings, but that phrase does not necessarily preclude follow-up calls after you've applied; the phrase is generally intended to discourage those who want to apply or ask questions over the phone during the initial resume-gathering process. Some exceptions exist, but most employers will accept follow-up phone calls in which, at the very least, you ask if the hiring manager has received your materials and inquire as to whether he or she has questions about your qualifications. Some employers, especially for sales-related positions, see your follow-up as a test of your persistence and interest in the job.

3. Parlay your inquiry into an opportunity to sell yourself and request an interview. Have a short sound bite prepared that relates your top selling points to the employer's needs. Be prepared for

the possibility that this phone call could turn into a short screening interview; read guidelines for screening and phone interviews in Chapter 4.

4. If you are uncomfortable with calling, e-mail is possible, though you will never know the e-mail's impact (or even if the addressee received it) unless the employer responds to it. Another trick is to call after hours and leave a message on the hiring manager's voicemail. That way your follow-up is nonintrusive and gives the decision-maker a choice about calling you back.

5. Don't make a pest of yourself, but don't just sit by the phone waiting for employers to call, either. You can enlist your network in your follow-up efforts. You could request that a contact who is an insider at your targeted organization query the hiring manager along these lines: "My friend Gloria, who turned around a real marketing fiasco at ZYX Corporation, applied for our senior marketing VP vacancy. I just wanted to make sure you got her application materials. I recommend you bring her in for an interview; she's super sharp."

(2)

Due Diligence: Research to Prepare for Every Interview Aspect

Research is one of the most valuable tools you can take into an interview, especially at the executive and senior levels. Lower-level candidates who are not highly knowledgeable on every aspect of an employer's operations, competitors, and customers might get a pass, but a senior-level interviewee will be expected to know about the employer and its needs in great detail. Those who conduct extra research can truly stand out.

"Candidates have to go the extra mile in terms of their due diligence," says executive career coach Cheryl Palmer, whose company is Call to Career. "With a glut of candidates in many fields, executives have to go above and beyond to distinguish themselves from the competition." That kind of distinction, Palmer notes, comes from "researching the company thoroughly and finding out what its pain points are and then coming up with solutions to meet the needs. Because companies hire people to solve problems, executives need to demonstrate that they are the solution to the company's problems," Palmer urges.

When asked about his litmus test of the minimal amount of company knowledge he would expect a candidate to possess in an executive employment interview, Josh Chernin, general manager at Web Industries, Marlborough, Mass., said he'd anticipate the interviewee would know the basics of the business, a few of the large customers, the five markets the company competes in, the company's divisions and their locations, the fact that the company is 100-percent employee-owned, and the number of employee-owners. "All of this is available on our Website except for the names of customers," Chernin says. Those can be obtained with a little second-rate sleuthing."

Chernin's test offers an overview of the most basic research expected of executive candidates, but the full scope of research includes the following:

- o The employer
  - o Brief history
  - o Products and services
  - o Organizational structure and key players
  - o Organizational culture
  - o Financials and financial health
  - o Key stakeholder groups
  - o Customers
  - o Competitors
  - o Geographic areas in which the employer operates
  - o Challenges, needs, issues, problems, and opportunities
  - o Recent news about the employer
- o The industry, including industry trends, especially if you are changing industries
- o Current events that affect the overall economic climate and how they impact the employer and industry in which you will interview
- o The geographic area in which your prospective workplace is located, if it represents relocation for you
- o The hiring manager/interviewer and any others who are likely to interview you

- o The requirements of the job you are interviewing for
- o The type of interview that the employer is likely to conduct (covered more fully in Chapter 4), along with the types of questions that are likely to be asked (Chapter 5)
- o Yourself
  - o Accomplishments and results
  - o Personality
  - o Skills, competencies
  - o Cultural fit with the employer and position
  - o Personal brand and top selling points

Twenty years ago, this level of comprehensive research would have required hours in a library. Today, you can easily use the Internet to conduct most of the research you need to prepare for an interview. You can fill in gaps by talking to members of your immediate and extended networks. With due diligence, this easy to execute. You really have no excuse not to fully prepare yourself.

Researching the employer

"Walk into every interview with a solid understanding of the company's product and/or services, competition, competitive advantage, weaknesses, size, revenues (if publicly held), mission, and corporate philosophy," advises career coach Robyn Feldberg, president of Abundant Success Career Services, Frisco, Tex. Palmer adds, "This type of information can help you come across as a truly motivated candidate as you integrate this knowledge into your questions that you ask of the interviewer at the end of the interview."

Researching the employer also helps you determine if you are a good fit. "Start with the big picture," advises author and career counselor Susan Guarneri of Guarneri Associates, Three Lakes, Wis., who suggests asking such questions as: "What is the culture of the company and the management team? Will it be a good fit with your values, leadership style, vision and mission, and personal brand? What are its current problems, both within the industry and the economy? Historically, how has it dealt with those problems? What needs to change?"

Once you've unearthed key employer information, Certified Employment Interview Coach Georgia Adamson, whose San Jose-based career practice is called A Successful Career, advises analyzing in terms of how you can uniquely position yourself for consideration based on your strengths, expertise, and past accomplishments—and how these attributes meet the employer needs you've uncovered in your research. Adamson notes that if you conduct the bulk of your research even before you submit your resume and cover letter, interview preparation becomes more of a refresher and opportunity for refinement "rather than a full-blown research project." Guarneri goes a step further, suggesting that you develop a short white paper making your case—in easy-to-read bullet points—for how you fit in and how you will meet employer needs. The paper could address company challenges, their causes, and your ideas for addressing them. This white paper can serve merely as a preparation tool for your own use—or you can turn it into a leave-behind to give to the interviewer at the end of the interview. For your own preparation, list questions you can ask in the interview to fill gaps where you lack enough information to address the employer's problems. In his book, *The Executive Job Search*, Orrin Wood suggests preparing a "failure analysis," in which you analyze reasons you could fail in your interview and then for each reason, list what you could do differently. Thus, you can take steps to avoid failure by doing things differently before they occur.

Know what's being said about the employer—and what it is saying about itself—in the media. Barb Poole, president of Hire Imaging, LLC, St. Cloud, Minn., recommends reading blogs, newspapers, white papers, and articles. "Go where your target audience is—offline and online—to learn about them and put yourself on their radar," Poole advises. "You will be armed with the inside information you need in an interview situation—to speak to their needs, challenges, pain, and victories." Guarneri suggests ferreting out this information through Internet keyword searches on search engines like Google, but also sites like BlogPulse (*www.blogpulse.com*), an automated trend-discovery system for blogs, and Technorati (*http://technorati.com),* a blog search engine. She also recommends WebMynd (*www.webmynd.com/ html*), a free extension for the Firefox Web browser that aggregates online information from multiple sources.

While most information you would want to research about an employer is online these days, two other sources can be useful. The first is members of your network, especially those who work or previously worked for your targeted employer or had any business dealings with the organization. Don't be shy about calling on them for information, as they can produce some of the most valuable insider intelligence. The second source is the company itself. It never hurts to call the company and request to have literature sent to you, especially if you already have an interview scheduled. While it's true that most company literature has an online counterpart, you never know when the company might send you a gem that offers unusual insight. You can also ask the company to send bios of the people you will interview with. In his book, *The Executive Rules*, Thad Greer recommends contacting someone in the targeted company's sales force because "most salespeople will tell you anything you want to know." A sales rep is an especially good resource for researching the important question of who the company's competitors are. Members of the media (including bloggers) who have covered your targeted employers can also be excellent information sources.

Consider conducting a SWOT analysis (the company's internal Strengths and Weaknesses, Opportunities and external Threats) on targeted employers. You might also craft a form on which to collect key information about each employer with whom you intend to interview.

More tools for researching employers are listed in the next section.

Key tools for conducting company research

Google: *www.google.com*. You can also set up a news alert through *news.google.com* to send you an e-mail every time news appears on the Web about a specific company, industry, or business topic.

The employer's Website. Most public companies have a section of their Website dedicated to investor relations and often provide their annual reports online and in downloadable form. You can also go to the Quintessential Directory of Company Career Centers at *www.quintcareers.com/career_centers* to find a link that takes you directly to the career section of the Website. At the employer's Website, Palmer advises making particular note of the organization's mission and vision statement "so you can be prepared to talk about how your personal values coincide with the vision statement." Company Websites usually have a section targeted at the press, where Palmer recommends locating media releases describing new initiatives the company is working on. The site's "About Us" section also should yield rich information.

Professional organizations and associations. See *www.quintcareers.com/ professional_organizations.html* for employer and industry intelligence.

Step-by-Step Guide to Researching Companies: *www.quintcareers.com/ researching_companies_guide.html.*

Researching Companies from the Career Development Center at Worchester Polytechnic Institute: *www.wpi.edu/Admin/CDC/research companies.html.*

Researching Companies on the Internet—A Tutorial: *www.learnwebskills.com/ company*, provides a step-by-step process for finding free company and industry info on the Web.

Thomas J. Long Business & Economics Library: *http://www.lib. berkeley.edu/BUSI/bbg4.html*, a guide to researching companies and industries from the Walter A. Hass School of Business, University of California, Berkeley.

Searching for Company Information: *www.nypl.org/research/sibl/company/ c2index.htm*, a guide to conducting basic research on U.S. and global companies.

LinkedIn Company Search: *www.linkedin.com/companies*, a research tool to help users explore and find the right companies to work for and do business with.

LinkedIn Answers: *www.linkedin.com/answers*, where you can ask questions about employers (as well as industries and jobs) and get answers from other members.

Glassdoor.com: *www.glassdoor.com/index.htm*, information about company salaries, reviews, and interviews for more than 23,000 companies, posted anonymously by employees.

IRIN—The Investor Relations Information Network: *www.irin.com/cgi-bin/main.cgi*, a clearinghouse of annual reports, fact books, and press releases.

MetaMoney.com: *http://metamoney.com/w100*, tracks the largest American and international companies on the Web (ranked by revenue), listing these corporations along with their Fortune500 and Global500 rankings.

Hoover's Online: *www.hoovers.com*, offers extensive company information, most of it by paid subscription.

Canadian Business Resource: *www.cbr.ca*, detailed profiles on more than 50 Canadian companies, with information available on more than 2,500 Canadian firms available by paid subscription.

CorporateInformation: *www.corporateinformation.com*, company research reports, primarily on financials, on more than 31,000 companies from more than 55 countries. Some free content; company research reports are by paid subscription.

Vault.com: *www.vault.com*, offers information on thousands of companies, some requiring paid membership.

Dun & Bradstreet's Million Dollar Database: *www.dnbmdd.com/mddi*, provides information by paid subscription on approximately 1.6 million U.S. and Canadian leading public and private businesses.

Wetfeet.com: *http://wetfeet.com/Employers*, short snapshots about companies.

Onesource.com: *www.onesource.com*, subscription-based global information on companies, industries and executives; also offers free company snapshots at *http://free.onesource.com/*.

Dow Jones' Factiva.com: *http://factiva.com*, subscription-based business news and information.

Standard & Poor's: *www2.standardandpoors.com*, fee-based financial market intelligence, including credit ratings, indices, investment research, risk evaluation, and data.

StockMarketYellowPages.com: www.*stockmarketyellowpages.com*, free news, stock quotes, and forecasts searchable by sector or by business name.

The Public Register's Annual Report Service (PRARS): *www.prars.com*, includes the ability to order free printed versions of annual reports.

Forbes Largest Private Companies: *www.forbes.com/private500*, an annual ranking of the top private companies in the United States, including number of employees, sales ranking, and a brief company description.

The Inc. 500: *www.inc.com/inc500*, a listing and short description of the 500 fastest-growing, privately held companies in the United States.

Better Business Bureau: *www.bbb.org*, includes links to companies that are members of the organization.

Small Business Administration Library and Resources: *www.sba.gov/ tools/resourcelibrary/index.html*, offers a collection of information about business trends and small businesses.

Allstocks.com's World's Largest Investors Links: *www.allstocks.com/links*, provide links to diverse information about companies and industry analyses.

Valueline.com: *www.valueline.com*, a subscription-based service primarily relating to investments, but offering a Ratings & Reports section with one-page reports about approximately 1,700 companies and 98 industries.

US Securities and Exchange Commission Filings and Forms Edgar Database: *www.sec.gov/edgar.shtml*: Financial and operational reports that companies, foreign and domestic, are required to file with the SEC. Particularly helpful reports include 10-K (containing executive salary information and many contact names) and 10-Q reports.

Researching the industry

If you've reached the senior level and plan to stay in your current industry, your knowledge of that sector is likely sufficient. But if you plan to switch industries, you'll need to conduct comprehensive research on the new field. "Thoroughly research the trends, opportunities, and problems specific to the employer's industry," Feldberg urges, "and be prepared to speak to them." The following section lists resources for learning more about industries.

Key tools for conducting industry research

Fuld & Company: *www.fuld.com/Tindex/13.html*, an information source on a wide range of industries.

IndustryLink: *www.industrylink.com*, large collection of resources on 25 industries.

Industry Portals: *www.virtualpet.com/industry/mfg/mfg.htm*, a collection of industry portals for diverse industries.

Annual Survey of Manufacturers: *www.census.gov/mcd/asmhome.html*, U.S. Bureau of the Census site that provides sample statistical estimates for all manufacturing establishments with one or more paid employee.

MacRAE'S Blue Book: *www.macraesbluebook.com*, an industrial directory of more than 500,000 North American industrial companies.

Print resources on industries

U.S. Industry & Trade Outlook, McGraw-Hill

Standard & Poor's 500 Guide (annual editions), McGraw-Hill

Standard & Poor's Industry Surveys Guide (annual editions), McGraw-Hill

Almanac of Business and Industrial Financial Ratios (annual editions), CCH, Inc.

Annual Statement Studies, The Risk Management Association.

Researching the economic climate

The notion of researching the current economic climate may seem odd. After all, you are living in that climate, so you presumably are quite familiar with it. Unexpected cataclysmic events such as the financial meltdown of 2008, however, remind us that the climate is turbulent and ever changing. You will also want to be well-versed on how current economic conditions affect your targeted employers—and industries—if you seek to transition from one sector to another.

Executive career coach Beverly Harvey of HarveyCareers.com points out some of the recent business upheavals that have shifted the economic landscape: the accounting scandals that led to a series of spectacular corporate collapses while others survived unmarked; the dot-com bust that caused a downturn in all high-tech fields and subsequent two-year recession; the print publishing industry that's continually threatened by online publishing; the airline industry's volatility; and the many industries threatened by foreign imports.

In the face of the economic challenges your targeted employers and industry face, Harvey notes, you'll want to research ways you can highlight accomplishments you've had in keeping a company afloat or thriving during a difficult time.

As a senior executive, explain how you kept threatened companies afloat and how you positioned them as industry leaders despite the economic crisis. Explain the most difficult times the company experienced and showcase your contributions to the company's survival. Be sure you are on top of business and economic news, especially as it affects your targeted industry and employers. Trade publications, along with resources in the following section, can help.

Business news resources for researching the economic climate

Wall Street Journal: *WSJ.com*

CEOexpress.com: *ceoexpress.com/default.asp*

Boardroominsider.com: *www.boardroominsider.com*

Barron's Magazine: *www.barrons.com*

BizJournals: *www.bizjournals.com*

BusinessWeek: *www.businessweek.com*

Financial Times: *www.usa.ft.com*

Forbes: *www.forbes.com*

Fortune: *http://money.cnn.com/magazines/fortune*

HighBeam Research: *www.highbeam.com*

MSN Money: *moneycentral.msn.com*

USA Today: *www.usatoday.com*

Media Jumpstation: *www.directcontactpr.com/jumpstation*, links to many media outlets

MediaLinksNow.com: *www.medialinksnow.com*, links to publishers, catalogs, newspapers, magazines, and news organizations from around the world.

NewsDirectory: *newsdirectory.com*, links to newspapers and media in the U.S. and internationally.

NewsLink: *http://newslink.org*, links to major U.S. and international newspapers, magazines, and radio and television stations.

Lexis-Nexis Business: *www.lexisnexis.com*, resource for business news and company information. Requires access to library databases.

Researching the geographic area

If taking a job with a targeted employer will require relocation, the employer may well ask you what you know about the area, how you feel about relocating, and how you believe the company's location affects its operations. Research about the employer's location is especially crucial if it's outside your native country. Later, as you are weighing whether to accept an offer, your research about the area to which you would have to relocate will prove valuable. Resources in the next section will assist you in researching new areas.

Key tools for conducting geographic research

CIA World Factbook: *https://www.cia.gov/library/publications/the-world-factbook*, offers detailed snapshots, compiled by the U.S. government, of just about every country in the world.

CountryReports.org: *www.countryreports.org*, top-line information about just about every country worldwide, including culture, geography, economy, political system, news, maps, and more.

Country Studies: http:*//lcweb2.loc.gov/frd/cs/cshome.html*, guides from the U.S. Library of Congress cover social, economic, political, and national security systems and institutions of more than 100 countries throughout the world.

globalEDGE: *http://globaledge.msu.edu/ibrd/ibrd.asp*, a comprehensive global business resource center from Michigan State University.

Global Insight: *www.globalinsight.com*, provides comprehensive economic, financial, and political coverage of countries, regions, and industries available from any source—covering more than 200 countries and spanning more than approximately 170 industries.

International Business & Technology: *www.brint.com/International.htm*, a learning portal from BRINT Institute that provides links to business, communication, import-export, linguistic, legal, marketing, media, monetary, public affairs, research, technology, trade, and travel information at both world and country levels.

Sperling's BestPlaces.net: *www.bestplaces.net*, offers data, statistics, and comparisons about U.S. cities, counties, and foreign countries.

World Trade Organization: *www.wto.org*, source for worldwide business and trade information and trends.

Researching people with whom you will interview

Researching the people who will interview you is where talking with members of your network can be especially valuable, and that includes members of your online network. "It will be easier to build rapport if you already know something about your interviewers," Palmer says. Guarneri agrees that determining points of similarity between you and your interviewers will help you break the ice and build chemistry in the interview. Such points of similarity might include attendance at the same college, membership in the same professional organizations, and similar hobbies and interests. Don't overlook the important task of determining how to pronounce the names of everyone you'll interview with.

Palmer suggests using professional networking sites such as LinkedIn to find profiles of the people that you will interview with as well as some personal information about them—such as the schools they attended and other places where they worked. "Absolutely have a presence on LinkedIn," Poole advises. "You can often dodge the gatekeepers and make direct contact with the decision-makers." The following section offers resources for learning more about people.

Key resources for researching people

LinkedIn: *www.linkedin.com*, professional network with 40 million-plus members in more than 200 countries.

ZoomInfo: *www.zoominfo.com*, summarization search engine that finds and extracts current online information about people and companies.

Jigsaw: *www.jigsaw.com*, searchable database of millions of business contacts.

Pipl: *http://pipl.com*, search engine for finding people.

Facebook: *http://www.facebook.com*, social-networking venue with large membership.

Spock: *http://www.spock.com*, search engine for finding people.

123People: *www.123people.com*, search engine for finding people.

Google, *www.google.com*, the world's predominate search engine is effective for finding information about people.

Spoke: *www.spoke.com*, tool that enables connection with 55 million businesspeople at 2.3 million companies.

Harris Infosource Company Directory, book, available at libraries.

Researching the requirements of the job

In an interview, you can't tell an employer how well you meet the requirements of the job unless you know in great detail what those requirements are. You may have responded to an ad or job posting spelling out the requirements but probably not providing the full picture. If you've been sought out and vetted by a recruiter, he or she probably believes you meet the requirements, but you may still have more to learn about the qualifications for the job. Here are some ways to research the job requirements:

Contact the employer's HR department or the department in which the targeted job is contained and ask for a written job description. Keep in mind, however, that you may still need to read between the lines and conduct additional research.

Contact members of your network or members of networking groups such as LinkedIn who work for or have dealings with the employer (such as customers and suppliers) and ask them what they know about what it takes to succeed in the position for which you are interviewing.

If you are working with a recruiter, ask probing questions, such as these:

- o What is the employer really looking for? What are the employer's priorities?
- o Why is the position open? Is it a new position, or is the organization replacing someone? What happened to that person? What were the previous person's successes?
- o What are the opportunities and risks inherent in the position?
- o How financially healthy is the organization? What does future growth look like?
- o What is the employer's strategy and future plans?
- o How big is the organization?
- o How many people will you manage and in what locations?
- o What are its key markets, both geographical and in terms of products or services?
- o Is it a domestic company or international?

- o   What subsidiaries does it have, and where are they located?
- o   How much travel is required for the job?
- o   How does the company measure success in its executives?

In preliminary phone screenings with the employer, don't ask questions that could easily be answered through research, but ask diplomatically about why the position is open and qualities the employer seeks in the new hire. After all, the phone screening is just as much your opportunity to determine if the employer is right for you as it is for the employer to screen you.

Researching the type of interview that will be conducted

It's critical to your preparation to know as much as possible about the type of interview the employer will conduct because your preparation will vary widely from one type to another. Sometimes the employer or recruiter will provide great detail about the interview process; in other cases, you will need to ferret out information. The best approach is to contact the assistant to the person who will be interviewing you and ask about the interview format.

Questions to ask:

- o   What type of interview format will be used (for example, behavioral, situational, screening)?
- o   How much time should I block out in my schedule for the interview?
- o   With whom will I interview?
- o   Will any part of the interview be in a group or panel format?
- o   What should I plan to bring or prepare for the interview?
- o   Will any meals be involved in the interview process?

Once you have the answers, you can learn more about specific preparations in Chapter 4.

Vague responses or reluctance to respond could be a red flag—an indicator of a haphazard or poorly thought out interview process. If you proceed with that interview, you will probably want to be prepared to be proactive in steering the interview in a direction favorable to you. Read more about handling poor interviewers in Chapter 6.

Another resource is Glassdoor.com (*www.glassdoor.com/Interview/index.htm*), which enables users to learn about employers' interview and hiring processes, including actual questions for any job or company. Interviewees review their interview experiences and comment on how challenging the interview was.

Opportunities Missed When Research is Deficient

Speaker and author Rob Sullivan, founder of the site *RIFProofing.com*, tells a story of how solid research can keep opportunity from slipping through your fingers:

"One would hope that anyone at the executive level—or any level for that matter—would be smart enough to research a company as a normal part of his or her due diligence. Unfortunately, I have seen firsthand that what should be a given is often the exception. For an executive with even a moderate dose of initiative, that can be a huge opportunity.

"About five years ago, I was hired by a start-up online brokerage firm that specializes in options trading to screen candidates for a senior vice president, marketing, position. The first and most important responsibility for the SVP was to manage the online partner relationships with the goal of increasing the customer base. To give the applicants an opportunity to truly shine, I invited everyone to submit a detailed letter explaining why this position was the next logical step in his or her professional development. This letter was required for any applicant who wanted to be considered.

"Of the hundreds who originally applied, only 25 submitted letters. I wasn't particularly surprised about that, given how easy the Internet makes it for any idiot who feels like applying to apply. I set up phone interviews with all of the applicants.

"Although the company was a start-up, it was well-funded and had an incredibly robust Website and trading platform. That was part of what enabled it to grow to a $2 billion company in less than six years. Nevertheless, we still wanted to hear objective feedback from these senior marketing people about the Website. So, one of the first questions I asked was, 'What did you think of the site?'

"Unlike Charles Schwab or E*Trade, this company did not have offices all over the city. The only way you could get any information about the company was to visit the Website. In other words, you had to do a little homework. But that didn't happen. Of the 25 interviewees, only three had ever visited the Website! That is absolutely *horrifying*. I still don't understand how or why anyone would take the time to write a follow-up application without doing any research whatsoever.

"Of the three candidates who did visit the Website, a man named Chris provided a textbook example of how to properly approach the challenge. Chris imagined he already had the job and asked himself what he might do on his first day of work if no one was there to give him direction. First, he managed to find the current list of partners, something that wasn't listed prominently anywhere on the site. Once he had the names, he visited all of the partner sites and listed his observations and recommendations in a detailed spreadsheet. The whole process took him about an hour, but earned him an interview with the founder of the company. What a wonderful example of initiative and the power of research."

Researching yourself

The notion of researching yourself may strike you as bizarre. You are likely a mature professional at the senior or executive level—surely you know everything there is to know about yourself. But self-research is an often neglected aspect of interview preparation. Honest self-assessment might have prevented many high-profile executives from disastrous falls from grace in leadership positions. Even more important than comprehensive self-knowledge about your relevant characteristics is the ability to articulate those attributes in the interview. The better you know your accomplishments, personality, skills, values, and personal brand, the better you'll be able to communicate them to the interviewer. If you feel you need to know yourself better before interviewing and do not feel comfortable conducting an introspective process on your own, consider working with a career counselor or coach, who may conduct assessments on you. You may also find it helpful to learn how others perceive your personality and other professional attributes. A fee-based but inexpensive online tool for gathering this information is the 360°Reach Personal Brand Assessment (*www.reachbrandingclub.com/360.html*), which gathers feedback from anyone you designate about rational and emotional attributes, strengths, weaknesses, and more.

Accomplishments and results

A resume and cover letter that have resulted in getting you an interview are probably good indicators that you've successfully spelled out the accomplishments and measurable outcomes you've attained for past employers. Accomplishments detailed in terse resume language, however, are not the same as those clearly communicated verbally. You also may not have written your own resume but hired a professional resume writer, so the words in it that describe your achievements may not roll easily off your tongue.

Analyze your accomplishments very specifically to each position you plan to interview for. Identify the achievements most relevant to the targeted employer's priorities, needs, and challenges (which you've uncovered through your other research). To get to know your own accomplishments so you can talk about them effectively, identify the achievements most relevant to the position for which you're interviewing. You can find a tool for doing so, an Accomplishments Worksheet, here: *www.quintcareers.com/accomplishments_worksheet.html*.

Next, write concise stories about each accomplishment. Consider a Situation-Action-Result format, as discussed in greater detail in Chapter 5. Be sure to use recent examples and quantifiable results wherever possible. The purpose of this writing exercise is not to provide a script to memorize, but rather to train your brain to recall these accomplishment stories in a way that enables you to relate them with ease in the interview. Read over your stories several times and then practice telling them without the written versions in front of you. Be sure they sound natural, not memorized.

Personality

At the executive level, relevant personality aspects include, among many other variables, flexibility, leadership style, need for achievement, introversion versus extroversion, and locus of control. Adam Robinson, founder and CEO, Ionix Hiring Systems, in fact, calls locus of control a "foolproof" way to size up anyone. Candidates with an internal locus of control, Robinson says, take responsibility for results, both good and bad, while those with an external locus of control look to place the responsibility outside themselves. Introversion compared to extroversion is an issue at the executive level because many people perceive that introverts can't be good leaders (Jennifer Kahnweiler's recent book, *The Introverted Leader: Building on Your Quiet Strength,* argues the opposite viewpoint).

The task in knowing your personality is twofold—attaining self-knowledge that enables you to understand to what degree your personality will mesh with that of your interviewer and prospective colleagues, and the ability to make a case for aspects of your personality, like introversion, that interviewers may perceive negatively. If you have never undergone an assessment like the Myers-Briggs Type Indicator, you may want to do so before your next round of interviewing. Although you can find various free variations on the Myers-Briggs online, your best bet is to seek out a career counselor or coach trained in both interpreting this instrument and in job-interview preparation. He or she can guide you through the implications of your personality type for the interview process.

Skills and Competencies

By this time in your career, you are likely well familiar with your skills—both universal skills such as leadership, communication, teamwork, and problem-solving, as well as job- or industry-specific competencies. You would not have risen to your level without possessing and knowing these competencies and strengths. Scrutinizing yourself in preparation for interviewing, however, requires that you honestly assess your abilities. Identify any personal weaknesses in the skills required for the position for which you're interviewing. Also, ask yourself if you truly enjoy using all the skills required for the job. If you don't, you may want to think twice about pursuing the job or consider what adjustments and accommodations you could make once you're in the job—perhaps drawing on the skills of other members of your team.

Your understanding of your own skills will also be important if you are changing careers or industries in which a different skill set will be required from what you are accustomed to.

Scrutinize job postings or descriptions to identify the skills needed for the job for which you are interviewing. Then, truthfully assess the level to which you possess each skill. You may also want to ask former bosses, colleagues, and subordinates how they saw your skills in each area. You may be surprised that they view your skills very differently from the way you do.

If you are changing industries or job functions, carefully evaluate skills required for your prospective new area. Then develop vivid examples of how skills you've used during your past experience are directly transferable and applicable to the new field or functions.

Values and cultural fit with the employer and position

At your level, you know what you value in a position and the type of organizational culture with which you are comfortable in the workplace. Do you know how those values will fit in with any employer with whom you are considering interviewing? Have your values changed based on your experience, or are you changing careers or industries? You may need to reassess your values in light of your interview plans. A Values Checklist for doing so, developed by life coach Liz Sumner, is available at *www.quintcareers.com/ values_checklist.pdf.* You will also want to learn as much as you can about the culture of the workplaces you're considering. The company research outlined in this chapter can tell you something about the culture, but your best resource is your network—past and current employees of your targeted organizations, along with customers and suppliers. Understanding the culture will help you bolster your case for how you fit in—and learning that the culture is wrong for you can save aggravation in pursuing an employer.

Patty DeDominic, managing partner with DeDominic & Associates, a business-consulting firm, tells a story of how failure to know and understand an organization's culture ended an executive's candidacy. "We were recruiting a CEO for a Chamber of Commerce," DeDominic recalls. "One candidate was extremely smart, capable, and appeared qualified; however, his style was to refer to his board of directors as lay leaders. This approach may have worked in his religious professional background but was the wrong cultural message to try to send to a Chamber of Commerce, which is filled with servant leaders who mostly see themselves as community leaders and professional community builders—not laypersons. This language alone, which in my opinion demonstrated that he was unaware of the culture of the industry he was interviewing for, caused the candidate to be dropped out of the process early on," DeDominic explains.

Personal brand and top selling points

You learned in Chapter 1 that developing your personal brand at the outset of a job search provides a self-marketing framework for all your communication efforts in the search. Ensure that you truly know and are comfortable communicating your personal brand and top selling points—what distinguishes you from other candidates—as you conduct your interview due diligence. Poole preps her executive clients so they can brainstorm and inventory their brand relative to the frequent competencies desired for players at senior and C-levels. These competencies, Poole says, include influence and collaboration, strategic direction, market awareness, results focus, and change leadership. Here are Poole's guidelines for integrating and articulating these competencies as part of your brand:

o Be prepared to show how you can create partnerships and collaborative efforts at the highest level, how you can create innovative partnerships that not only span the organization, but reach beyond its walls.

o You must have a strategic plan relative to your potential employer's needs that integrates many business issues, functions, and resources for effective action. You also need to describe how you executed strategically for previous employers.

o   You must know the market well enough to anticipate, capitalize on, and potentially drive market changes.

o   Not only must you meet/exceed goals, but you must also introduce improvements that pave the way for higher goals. You also should be able to transform a business for significantly improved results.

o   You should be able to mobilize individuals or groups to change. Ideally, you will be skilled at creating massive coordinated change across an entire complex organization.

3

Nonverbal Interview Preparation

The content of what you say in response to questions—and the content of questions you ask (as covered in Chapter 5)—is obviously exceedingly important in a job interview. What is less well-known is the importance of the part of the interview that isn't spoken—the way you present yourself and behave nonverbally. Your nonverbal preparation is literally the unspoken secret of job interviewing.

If you think nonverbal behavior can't sink an interview, here's a story that might change your mind. In a past job, my boss asked me to screen applicants to fill a vacancy in our department and narrow the pool down to three finalists. I did so, and my boss then interviewed the trio. When I asked him his impressions of the candidates, he said he had already eliminated one of them because the candidate never made eye contact during the entire interview.

In fact, "Many communication experts say that as much as 90 percent of what we say comes from nonverbal cues, including our body language," says Barb Poole, president of Hire Imaging, LLC, St. Cloud, Minn. Career consultant Ford R. Myers, president of Career Potential, LLC, in Haverford, Penn. agrees: "More attention is paid to how your body communicates—body language—than is paid to your verbal communication. Our body language in the work environment speaks volumes and ... the most important time to consider what your body is saying is during the job interview," Myers says. "How your body acts during this all-important meeting sets the tone for hiring decisions, as well as future interactions with superiors and co-workers. The impact of a great resume and impeccable references is greatly diminished if your body language and physical presence don't meet the interviewer's expectations. So, always be aware of how your body communicates," he advises.

Let's look at each nonverbal factor individually:

Interview attire and grooming. A surprising number of hiring managers interviewed for this book said that the executive-level candidates they interview often display poor or inappropriate attire or grooming.

A few simple guidelines can help you make sure you outfit yourself appropriately for an interview:

- o Err on the side of conservatism. Candidates are often advised to dress in the manner of other employees in the organization in which they are interviewing, but hiring managers have been saying recently, especially at the executive and senior levels, that they want to see candidates dress in the most conservative, authoritative business attire (not business casual). That means a matching jacketed suit for both men and women, conservative colors (such as black, gray, and navy, though women can usually get away with a broader range of colors), polished shoes (closed-toed, low-to-medium-heeled shoes for women), and ties for men. Though I've been branded a throwback and stared at in jaw-dropping disbelief, I recommend skirted suits for women for first interviews simply based on the "err on the side of conservatism" rule. A pantsuit will always carry an ever so slight element of risk with an old-school, conservative interviewer. Blouses and shirts should be in light colors. The monochromatic look in which a suit, shirt, and tie are all of the same dark color, makes men look like gangsters.

o Be sure your clothing fits properly—not too tight, too baggy, or too low-cut for women. Ensure that your shirt color, size, and sleeve length are appropriate. Be aware that a well-tailored outfit can minimize imperfections in your body shape. If you are unsure of what looks good on you, shop in stores that offer personalized service and let the sales associates assist you with the proper fit, including tailoring to improve the fit.

o Have your hair professionally cut and/or styled and keep your hair neat and off your face. One of my pet peeves as an interviewer is seeing hairstyles that obscure my view of the candidate's face. Especially in a panel interview, remember that interviewers may see your face in profile, so hair should not block that view.

o Less is more when it comes to makeup, jewelry, and especially fragrance. Tone down these enhancements. Fragrance should be at a bare minimum or omitted completely because your interviewer could be allergic. Don't overwhelm your interviewer with scent.

o At the same time, don't stink! Avoid bad breath and body odor (but don't chew gum or suck on a mint in the interview). Another odor that can be damning in an interview is of cigarettes. If you smoke, you are probably not aware that others can tell just from the way your clothes and body smell. Rita Ashley points out in her book, *Job Search Debugged*, that smokers are seen as lacking self-control, less intelligent than others in the face of the overwhelming evidence of smoking's effect on health, and more prone to take sick days. She advises laundering and separate storage for a smoker's interview clothing to minimize the smell.

o Watch your grooming. Be sure your fingernails are clean and your nose hair is trimmed. Although neat facial hair (beard, mustache) is only minimally risky for men, five 'o clock shadow is a turnoff.

o A picture is worth a thousand words. An excellent resource for interview attire is Syms' The Complete Interview Outfit for Women (*symsdress.com/womensfirst.htm*) and The Complete Interview Outfit for Men (*symsdress.com/mensfirst.htm*), which show photos of appropriate interview attire.

Items to bring to the interview. Be sure to bring several copies of your resume. The interviewer may have misplaced his or her copy, and you may also interview with multiple people who don't all have copies of your resume. Consider bringing a portfolio that will enable you to visually present examples of skills and accomplishments. (Read more about using a portfolio in your interview in Chapter 5. You might also bring a briefcase or attache case, but if you bring a portfolio, you may want to skip this extra baggage. That's especially true for women, who will likely be carrying a purse as well (although some experts advise against bringing a purse). Bring a small notepad and pen; most interviewers don't mind if you take notes as long as you maintain focus and don't jot your notes in a distracting way. Some interviewers, in fact, expect you to take notes. A good way to find out how your interviewer feels is to ask: "Do you mind if I take notes?" Because you will likely bring your cell phone to the interview, be sure it is turned off or on the silent setting before you enter the interviewer's office.

Facial expressions. The default job-interview facial expression is your smile. "A broad grin works wonders to convey that you are eager, confident and pleasant to work with," Poole says. Sure, there will be times in the interview when a smile is not appropriate. "Don't smile too broadly when discussing serious subjects, of course," Poole advises. Smiling throughout most of the meeting, though, is key to showing your enthusiasm. One of interviewers' top complaints about interviewees is that they fail to show sufficient enthusiasm; a smile is the best way to show how much you want the job. A warm smile is especially important when you first meet your interviewer.

Handshake and walk into the office. Your handshake should be confidently firm, but not bone-crushing. "As important as the grip tightness in the handshake," Poole notes, "is the palm-to-palm contact. It expresses an intention of honesty and openness, and that your interaction will be sincere and nonthreatening." Avoid the "limp fish" handshake.

Also consider adapting your handshake to your interviewer's. "While most people think that eye contact and hand gestures are important they do not realize that in addition, the 'skin in the game' is how to manage the handshake," notes Judy Rosemarin, president of Sense-Able Strategies, Inc., New York City. "All interviewees should sense the strength and style of the interviewer's kind and then adjust to it. So, if your handshake tends to be on the stronger side, and your interviewer's is softer, in a nanosecond, adjust your pressure to less strong. Nothing is said, but the feeling experienced by the interviewer is, "oh, he or she got me! The candidate is noticing me! This is a subtle way of honoring of the other," Rosemarin explains.

Be sure your palms are dry, not sweaty or clammy; use a handkerchief on them right before the interview, or try Moisture Absorb (*http://by142.com/products/moisture_ABSORB.html*) a product recommended in Oprah Winfrey's *O Magazine*. Make eye contact and smile as you shake hands.

You'll be standing at this point and ready to walk into the interviewer's office or other room in which the interview will be conducted. Walk tall—purposefully, confidently, and carrying yourself with conviction.

Sometimes forgotten in discussions of interview handshakes is the exit handshake at the end of the interview. If the interviewer offers his or her hand, you won't have trouble remembering the exit handshake, but if a hand isn't offered, extend yours. The exit handshake is a classy and professional gesture.

Posture. Once the interviewer invites you to take a seat, sit up straight. Good posture projects energy. Try the psychological trick of sitting slightly toward the edge of the chair to appear eager. This technique of leaning a bit toward the interviewer "can indicate that you're a gracious listener" as well as "interested, engaged and enthusiastic," Poole says, while cautioning not to lean so far into the interviewer's space as to risk decreasing his or her comfort level.

"Leaning back in your chair gives the impression you're dispassionate about the position," Poole cautions. My partner, Dr. Randall Hansen, learned the dangers of leaning back when a recruiter critiqued his interview performance after a job interview, informing him that he probably would not be considered for the job because he sat back in the chair in a too-relaxed manner. Be aware also, as Poole observes, "posture can be a sign of dominance or submissiveness. Calculate the image you want to portray. You will no doubt want to come across as not projecting too much of either."

Eye contact. As we've already seen, eye contact is extremely important because it helps you engage the interviewer, establish rapport, and contribute to the interactivity of the interview. "Interviewees who don't maintain eye contact come off unfocused and overly nervous," observes Ken Heisler, director of SALO Search, LLC, Minneapolis, Minn. "Be confident in your approach, and even if it makes you uncomfortable, look the interviewer in the eye as much as possible," Heisler advises. For Jessica Neill, a recruiter with Manpower in Zeeland, Mich, failure to make eye contact "appears shifty, and it makes the interviewer believe that you are either lying, or that you have not prepared for the interview and are insecure about your answers."

Some experts advise looking at the interviewer's nose or the space between his or her eyebrows to avoid the creepiness of keeping your eyes affixed on his or her eyes. In a panel interview, look at the questioner when responding to a question, but also glance at the other interviewers. "Eye contact varies in cultures; however, in the U.S., it means honesty and forthrightness," Poole says. "It's a good rule to actively look the interviewer(s) in the eyes—not only when they are speaking, but when you are speaking as well."

Hand gestures. It's fine to use hand gestures in a job interview. In fact, Poole advises interviewees to "animate just enough." Keep gestures small, contained, and close to your body. Poole tells of a hiring manager who studies body language and asserts that "a more complex gesture of two hands above the waist reflects complex thinking and gives the listener confidence in that speaker." Poole points to leaders such as Barack Obama, Bill Clinton, and other charismatic speakers who punctuate sentences with a hand gesture. "There is great power in effective hand gestures," Poole observes.

If you know you tend to get wildly carried away with hand gestures—or if nerves make your hands shake—try firmly holding a pen. When one of my students did that in a mock interview, I was amazed at how poised she looked.

Bad habits and inappropriate body language. Any number of quirky tics in an interview can derail your performance, and the worst problem is you may not even be aware you're exhibiting those behaviors. In a panel interview, I once had an interviewee who swept his hand back and forth across the table at which he was seated for the entire interview. Another sniffed loudly and nervously throughout the session. Both were unaware of what they were doing.

The interviewee who brushed the table illustrates the pitfalls of interviewing while sitting at a table or close to a desk, where nerves might provoke you to tap or drum your fingers on the surface, and a too-relaxed manner might cause you to lean or prop your elbows up on the table. If seated at a table, keep your hands free for small hand gestures, and when you're listening to the interviewer, fold your hands, lay them flat on the table, or hold a pen. Avoid crossing your arms, which Poole says, "makes you appear guarded and unapproachable—almost defensive."

Other typical inappropriate behaviors include leg shaking, fidgeting, twirling in a swivel chair, and playing with hands—and many interviewers have seen far worse. Most of these behaviors are the result of nerves. In her book *Interview Magic*, Susan Britton Whitcomb suggests channeling nervous energy by digging your index fingernail into the flesh of your thumb on the same hand.

"Legs wide open and arms stretched out can indicate that you're comfortable with who you are," Poole points out. "However, taking up too much space can be perceived of as thoughtless or arrogant. Take up less space by bringing your legs and arms closer to your torso and sitting up straighter in your chair for a more professional presence," Poole suggests. Also be aware of cultural preferences about personal space. While Americans prefer a couple of feet of personal space that we don't want others to violate, members of some other cultures see conversation partners as rude if they are not in each others' faces.

The most difficult nonverbal problem is profusely sweating because it is very hard to avoid and deal with once in the interview. If you are prone to extreme sweating, first see if your doctor has suggestions. And be sure to take a tissue or handkerchief into the interview; you may have to subtly blot sweat off your brow or face. My partner once saw a guy in an interview wipe sweat off his hand by running it through his hair (not a good idea).

Confident voice projection and avoiding verbal tics. Technically, these are not exactly nonverbal behaviors since they involve speech, but because they do not relate to interview content, they're included here. The best way to demonstrate confidence—a hugely important interview factor—is to project your voice strongly. Avoid a weak, high-pitched, timid, or baby-soft voice. Among the verbal tics to avoid:

o Pause words and phrases, such as uh, ah, um, like, you know. These are hard to avoid for many of us, but practice, preparation for responding to frequently asked interview questions, and taking a few seconds to gather your thoughts before responding can help.

o Trailing off at the end of a response. You can almost hear the ellipses (...) at the end of this kind of response. The candidate sounds like he or she isn't finished, yet stops speaking. Be sure you end your responses definitively.

o Raising your voice in a questioning manner or speaking in a sing-song rhythm. We might characterize these as the "Valley

Girl" way of speaking. The best way to avoid these habits is to be aware of them and practice speaking in a normal cadence.

o   Speaking too quickly or slowly.

What's the best way to ensure all your nonverbals make a great impression and you look right for the interview? Here are three suggestions:

1.   Engage in a mock interview or role play in which your interviewer focuses entirely on and critiques your nonverbals. You can do this mock interview with a career counselor or coach, but in a pinch, a family member or friend should do just fine.

2.   "Practice in the mirror until your body language looks natural," Poole advises.

3.   Have yourself videorecorded in a mock interview. This technique is especially useful for uncovering those tics and behaviors you may not be aware of. You may be amazed to see how you present yourself. Ideally you'll be amazed in a good way.

Remember that there is much more to preparing for an interview than practicing how you will respond to the questions. Consider the complete package and ensure that the nonverbal impression you present is as polished as is your content.

(4)

What Kind of Interview?

Knowing how to prepare for any type of employment interview will give you a major edge because significant variations in interview formats dictate different kinds of preparation. Because you may not always be able to determine what kind of interview you will experience, it's helpful to know something about all formats and be ready for them.

Job interviews can be categorized in several ways. The format of the interview refers to the time in the hiring process during which it takes place, the personnel involved in the interview, the interview's purpose, its focus, its style, its structure (or lack thereof), and its requirements of the candidate. Interview formats include:

- o Interview with recruiter/search firm
- o Screening/phone interview
- o First face-to-face interview
- o Second and subsequent face-to-face interviews

- o   Interview over a meal
- o   Panel interview
- o   Board of Directors interview
- o   Presentation interview
- o   Remote interview via video
- o   Work-assignment/simulation/problem-solving interview
- o   Stress interview

Another way to categorize interviews is by the nature of the content of the questions asked. Although many interviewers focus on just one type or style of content, others deploy a combination of content approaches. Examples of content types include:

- o   Traditional/screening questions
- o   Behavioral questions
- o   Case questions
- o   Situational questions
- o   Industry-specific questions
- o   Off-the-wall questions
- o   Illegal/inappropriate questions
- o   Combination of multiple question types

Significant overlap occurs among interview formats and content types. For example, a screening or phone interview could consist of traditional/screening questions, but it could also feature behavioral or situational questions. A panel interview could comprise behavioral questions, as well as industry-specific questions.

Finally, any interview format and any content type can be either structured or unstructured.

If we look at a matrix of interview formats and content types, we can see the many possibilities for overlap. Solid dots (●) indicate types of questions with a high probability of being asked; open dots (o) indicate types of questions with a lower probability of being asked:

Type of Content Question

Format	Traditional/ Screening	Behavioral	Case	Situational	Industry Specific	Off-the-wall	Illegal/ Inappropriate Question
Interview With Recruiter/ Search Firm	●	●	O	●	●	O	O
Screening/ Phone Interview	●	O	O	O	O	O	O
First Face-to-Face Interview	●	●	O	●	●	O	O
Second, Subsequent Face-to-Face Interviews	O	●	O	●	●	O	O
Interview Over a Meal	●	●		●	●	O	O

Type of Content Question

Format

	Traditional/ Screening	Behavioral	Case	Situational	Industry Specific	Off-the-wall	Illegal/ Inappropriate
Panel Interview	●	●		●	●	○	○
Board of Directors Interview	○	●	●	●	●	○	○
Presentation Interview	○	○	○	○	○	○	○
Remote Interview via Video	●	●		●	●	○	○
Work Assignment/ Simulation/ Problem Solving	○	○	●	○	●	○	○
Stress Interview							

Let's examine the characteristics of the various interview formats, content types, and structures—and the strategies for preparing for each one.

Overview of interview formats

Interview with recruiter/search firm

As we saw in Chapter 1, it's common for executive- and senior-level candidates to be sought out by and work with recruiters and executive-search consultants. These professionals frequently interview candidates as a prelude to sending them on to interview with their client employers (or deciding not to send them if the recruiter finds the candidate is not a good fit). As with initial interviews with employers, early interviews with recruiters are often conducted by phone. Recruiters also coach candidates and conduct practice interviews with them before the employer interview and debrief them intensely afterwards.

An interview with a recruiter is just as important as an interview with an employer. In fact, "the way you handle this interview determines whether you will meet the client [employer]," notes the book *Executive Search and Your Career* by the Association of Executive Search Consultants. Strive, therefore, to make your best impression. Prepare just as you would for an employer interview. Dress professionally and compose your thoughts on responding to the questions you might be asked. Plan to find out from the recruiter as much as you can about the employer you hope to interview with and the position, using the questions in Chapter 2. Realize that in the early stages, the recruiter may not reveal all the information you seek about the employer, but expect more information if the recruiter plans to send you to meet with the hiring organization. Be completely honest and open with the recruiter, and don't withhold information (such as your current and expected compensation). Project confidence, but not arrogance. Be prepared to give examples that substantiate your accomplishments and results. Once the recruiter decides you should interview with the employer, let him or her represent you. Don't contact the employer directly except to send a thank-you letter after the interview. See more about working with recruiters in the interview process in Chapter 6.

Screening/phone interview

Screening interviews are often the first interviews conducted in the hiring process. Mid-level staff people, such as personnel from an organization's human resources department or a subordinate to the hiring manager, may conduct these interviews, although hiring managers conduct them as well. As the name implies, screening interviews are intended to help the employer decide whether you should remain in the candidate pool and move on to the next phase of interviewing.

Questions asked in a screening interview are often very traditional queries found on lists of frequently asked interview questions. See more about screening questions in Chapter 5. Adam Robinson, founder and CEO of Ionix Hiring Systems, recommends a specific process and set of questions to enable employers to make a "go-no go" decision on moving a candidate forward. Robinson wants to know the candidate's career plan to ensure there's not a significant discrepancy between the interviewee's plan and the open position. Then he asks what the candidate is best at and what does he or she not like to do. For the "best at" skill, Robinson wants to hear a core competency of the open position. Robinson says it's important to identify the "don't like" skill, because "nothing else matters if you're offering a job the candidate doesn't want to do or isn't very good at doing." Robinson then goes through the candidate's job history, focusing on what former bosses would say about the candidate's performance. Finally he initiates a discussion of the open position and asks whether the candidate sees a good fit.

If your screening interview is with a human resources professional or anyone other than the person you will ultimately report to in this job, take it just as seriously and put as much effort into it as you would an interview with your next boss. In Chapter 7, professionals who conduct screening interviews detail their peeves with executives who are arrogant or impatient with screening interviewers. Undoubtedly, candidates have lost opportunities for projecting the wrong attitude in these interviews.

Sometimes interviewees are asked to take assessments as part of a screening interview. See more about these in Chapter 6.

Be sure to ask questions as part of a screening interview because the interview is just as much your opportunity to screen the employer as it is for the employer to screen you. See more about asking questions and sample questions to ask in Chapter 5. Employers frequently conduct screening interviews by phone. Especially if face-to-face interviews will involve travel, employers seek to reduce costs by winnowing the field and avoiding travel expenses for this early stage of interviewing. Some companies—as a cost-saving measure—are now using phone calls for more intensive interviews later in the interview process.

In some ways, you may find phone interviews easier and less stressful than face-to-face interviews. You can wear what you want and have all your resources in front of you, such as your resume and information about the employer. In other ways, phone interviews are more nerve-racking than face-to-face interviews because you cannot pick up on the interviewer's nonverbal cues (for that reason, be sure to *listen* especially carefully). Here are some guidelines for phone interviews that have helped others:

- o If you are inexperienced with phone interviews, or don't communicate extensively by phone in your current job, consider doing a practice interview with a career counselor, coach, or friend.

- o Find out when scheduling the interview how much time it will require so you can allot sufficient time.

- o Even though you *could* wear a ratty bathrobe for the phone interview, dressing nicely will help you project confidence and professionalism. Of course you don't have to dress as professionally as you would to interview face to face, but a business-casual outfit will help you feel great about yourself.

- o Assemble all the materials you might need to refer to both to talk about yourself and to talk about and ask questions about the employer—but review them thoroughly before the interview and don't depend on them as a crutch. You don't want to be heard rustling through papers and taking long pauses while looking up information to help you respond to a question; nor do you want to sound as though you are reading from your materials. Preparing key points on notecards is ideal because you can access them easily without fumbling and rustling. Have materials handy to write with as well so you can jot down points you want to remember about the interview.

- o Be sure you conduct the interview in a quiet place free of distractions, such as barking dogs or clamoring children. Make sure it's a place where you can focus and spread out your reference materials. Similarly avoid sniffling, sneezing, or coughing; excuse yourself if you can't avoid these behaviors. Obviously, don't eat, drink, or chew gum during the interview (though water right before is a good idea to keep your mouth from going dry).

o Ensure that you can hear and are being clearly heard. Use a landline if possible as it usually offers a clearer connection, but realize the interviewer may be using a cell phone. If the connection is terrible and makes communication impossible, suggest rescheduling the interview.

o Prepare for silences. The interviewer could be jotting down notes or not quite ready to ask the next question. Don't feel you need to fill in airtime. If the next question isn't forthcoming, ask a question related to your last response.

o Smile as much as you can during the interview. Even though the person on the other end of the phone can't see your smile, you will project warmth and enthusiasm if you smile. Judy Rosemarin, president of Sense-Able Strategies, Inc., New York City, suggests you interview in front of a mirror so you can see yourself smiling and projecting your interest in the job.

o If you tend to be nervous, consider standing and even walking around during the interview. I confess that phone interviews are my one downfall in the interview process; they unnerve me inordinately. My husband, who does excellent phone interviews, taught me to walk around during a phone interview to channel nervous energy, and my performance has improved significantly since I've started to move around.

o Remember that your goal is to advance to the in-person interview, so look for opportunities to suggest that you could offer even more details or show materials in person to demonstrate skills and accomplishments.

o Send a thank-you note afterwards. This recommendation applies to *every* interview at every stage of the process. See Chapter 7 for more on thank-yous.

First face-to-face interview

As disheartening as it may be, your first face-to-face interview almost definitely will not result in an offer. "The purpose of an interview is to get the next interview," Rosemarin says, "No executive ever gets hired after only one."

From the hiring decision-maker's perspective, the initial face-to-face interview is "the first opportunity that you as a hiring manager have to really dig into a person's background and experience with the goal of understanding whether or not they'll likely be a match for your position," Robinson says. As opposed to the telephone-screening interview, Robinson says the first interview is about the "big picture." Because the first face-to-face interview is your most significant opportunity to make the right impression and move to the next interview, let's spend some time looking at all the elements that make up that impression.

Through Chapter 2, you prepared yourself with all the background information you'll need to meet the employer. Chapter 3 prepared you to make the right nonverbal impression, and Chapter 5 will prepare you to respond to interview questions—so let's look at all the other aspects of the first face-to-face interview. Remember, too, that all these elements apply to subsequent interviews as well.

Call the interviewer's assistant to confirm your interview appointment a day or two before. If the interview is local, and you don't know how to get there, consider asking the assistant for directions. Another approach, of course, is to use a GPS device in your vehicle (or rental vehicle if the interview's not local) or get directions from a site such as Mapquest or Google Maps. Whichever you choose, be sure you know exactly where it is and how long it takes to get there (some GPS devices will tell expected arrival time once you program in your destination). If you have a poor sense of direction and often get lost when driving to new places, you might even consider taking a practice run to the interview location. That way, you'll know exactly where the interview location is and how long it takes to get there. On the actual interview day, allow extra time for traffic, road construction, or bad weather.

Get a good night's sleep the night before this potentially grueling day. Also, look for opportunities to refresh yourself during the interview day. If there's a break in the action, splash some water on your face or take a brisk walk to rejuvenate. You might want to take along a pocket- or purse-sized snack in case there is no lunch break. Breath spray, mints, or a mini-bottle of mouthwash are not a bad idea. Be careful not to run out of steam toward the end of the day. Maintain your energy, confidence, and enthusiasm.

Plan to arrive about 10-15 minutes early (any earlier and you may annoy the interviewer and staff). Your early arrival sets up your ability to quickly establish rapport with the interviewer once you meet. Be respectful, friendly, and warm with the receptionist, the interviewer's assistant, and any other support staff you meet. A major peeve of hiring decision-makers is the candidate who treats these staffers poorly. Chatting up—not too excessively—support staff and prospective coworkers serves the dual purpose of giving you a better feel for how much you'd like to be part of this workplace culture, as well as making a positive impression on as many people as possible.

Many career experts are now recommending a consultant mindset for interviews. In their book, *For Executives Only*, Bill Belknap and Helene Seiler advise adopting "a mindset that you are the world's greatest consultant. You are only there to tell them what is right for this organization, not what is right for you." Susan Britton Whitcomb, in *Interview Magic*, discusses "collaborating" with the interviewer on how the open job needs to be done. "A strategic, high-level conversation," is how Thad Greer characterizes this mindset in his book, *Executive Rules*. Rosemarin says "the interview is about solving the interviewer's needs and nightmares."

Why the consultant mindset and the focus on the employer rather than you, the candidate? You will be less nervous if the focus is off you and you think of yourself as a knowledgeable, powerful—even heroic—consultant who is there to help the employer meet needs, conquer challenges, and solve problems. You become less focused on selling yourself, and you don't appear desperate for a job. Any discomfort you feel in talking about yourself is diminished. You are not only helping the employer solve organizational issues, but also assisting the interviewer with the hiring decision.

Listen for clues that get at the heart of what the employer seeks in the person hired for this position and key into the needs, concerns, issues, and problems that you would be expected to handle.

Don't be afraid to pause for a few seconds before responding to a question; it's better to gather your thoughts than blurt out an inarticulate response. Other ways to buy a bit of time include repeating the question back to the interviewer or asking the interviewer to repeat the question.

Don't be surprised if your interview is actually a series of interviews—in both individual and group/panel formats—making for a long day. (Ideally, you will have determined ahead of time whether to expect multiple interviews.) You may interview with senior executives, department heads, and prospective team members. You may also get a tour of the workplace and be taken out to eat. If you see that a workplace tour is not included on the agenda, ask if someone can show you around as time permits. Plan to bring ample copies of your resume for all the people you may be meeting with.

Prepare plenty of questions to ask. See Chapter 5.

Collect the business card of everyone you meet with. Keep your small notepad handy to write down names in case there's someone from whom you can't get a card.

Take steps to "close the sale" in your final (or only) interview of the day. As mentioned, closing the deal in a first interview almost certainly doesn't mean getting the offer. It means expressing your enthusiasm for the position and asking about the next step in the process. See more about closing the interview in Chapter 5.

Second and subsequent face-to-face interviews

It's gratifying to be called for a second or subsequent interview because you are another step closer to the job. Pat yourself on the back for being called for a second interview. While some career experts say your chances are 1 in 4 to get the job at this point, others say you have as much as a 50 percent chance. Even with the field narrowing, it's important to distinguish yourself and ensure that you stand out above your competition.

Everything about second and subsequent interviews can be encapsulated in the word "more." Compared to the first interview, a later interview will likely involve more preparation, more people, more questions, more intensity, and more pressure—in addition to more likelihood that you will land the job. "The second interview is where we attempt to poke around inside the candidate's head and find out what makes them tick," Robinson says.

Don't neglect to review your performance from your first interview. See the post-mortem section in Chapter 7, and the Post-Mortem Survey at *http:// www.quintcareers.com/interview_post-mortem.pdf.* Note any questions or situations that caused you difficulty and plan how you will handle those aspects better in the second interview. Derive confidence from knowing that if you hadn't performed well in the first interview, you wouldn't have landed the second. Think about what made you shine in the first interview, and plan to do more of the same. Brainstorm new information you can bring into the second interview—new accomplishments, new examples, new evidence of how much you know about the employer.

Prepare even more than you did for the first interview. You researched the employer before the first interview; now it's time to delve even deeper into that research. Consult Chapter 2 for any areas you may have overlooked. Some experts suggest that talking with company insiders is one of the most productive ways to prepare for a second interview. Before your second interview, consider conducting informational interviews with company folks who aren't among those who'll be interviewing you. (To learn more about informational interviews, see the Informational Interviewing Tutorial at *www.quintcareers.com/informational_interviewing.html*). Be sure you're up to date on news of the employer and developments in your field or industry by reviewing Websites and trade publications.

Like the first interview, second and subsequent interviews may consist of multiple interviews. Continue to keep yourself apprised of what the agenda will be and with whom you can expect to interview. Don't slack off with your interview attire. A second interview generally doesn't denote a more casual interview.

A major reason for second and subsequent interviews is so the employer can see how well you fit in with the company culture. Put yourself inside the employer's head and realize that the interviewers at your second interview want to learn how well you will get along with other team members with whom you'll be interacting every day. Deploy your very best interpersonal communication skills. Keep in mind the idea of showing your fit—but remember that it's okay not to fit. If you aren't a good fit with the employer, you probably wouldn't be happy there. And remember that each interview is also your opportunity to determine whether the company is a good fit for you. Think about whether you would accept it if the employer extended an offer.

You may be asked some of the same questions you were asked in the first interview, but some new ones as well and some that are more complex and require you to dig more deeply for your responses. Second-interview questions may delve more into your personality, or they may be more targeted toward specific technical and industry-specific knowledge—or both. Plan to keep your responses fresh yet consistent for each person you meet with during later interviews, and don't worry about repeating yourself because you will likely have a different audience every time you give roughly the same response.

If you've obtained the full list of interviewers beforehand, a good way to keep your answers fresh is to try to find out something about each interviewer and tailor your response specifically to that person. You can also vary your delivery to freshen your responses. Interviewing expert Carole Martin suggests that a good way for the interviewer to get to know about your personality is through the quotes of others; for example, tell the interviewer what your boss would say about you if asked.

Don't be shocked if some of the people you meet with aren't very competent interviewers. While decision-makers trained in interviewing often conduct first interviews, the array of people who might talk with you during the second interview experience may include people lacking skills and training in how to manage an interview. Learn more about how to handle poor interviewers in Chapter 6.

Realize that you have some degree of control if the interview process drags on after a series of interviews.

Interview over a meal

Meals are often part of the interview process, especially at the executive level and especially as the process moves into second, third, and later interviews. The most important aspect of an interview over a meal is that it is still an interview. You and the interviewer (and others) may be seeking refreshment and sustenance, but you will still be under scrutiny at all times. Thus, remember not only all the principles of effective interviewing, but also the rules of etiquette and common sense. Your dining companions will observe your manners, poise, conversation skills, and judgment. Be sure you know proper dining etiquette and order a light meal that is not messy. Avoid pastas and sloppy sauces, along with anything that comes in a shell, such as lobster or crab. Even entrees such as chicken that must be cut from the bone can be dicey. Avoid foods such as garlic that will affect your breath. It's best not to order the most expensive item on the menu.

A few words about alcoholic beverages at a meal interview: Hiring decision-makers interviewed for this book were sharply divided on this subject. Some said a cocktail or glass of wine is okay if your interviewer is also indulging. Some said your having a drink depends on the employer's organizational culture, revealed through your research. The most sensible answer seems to replicate attire guidelines. Chapter 3 advised erring on the side of conservatism with your interview attire. The same goes for alcohol in a meal interview; err on the side of conservatism and making the safe choice—which means declining to imbibe. Certainly do not order alcohol if no one else does or you are the first to order. Lots of good reasons support this teetotaling approach. Alcohol could impair your judgment and delivery in the interview. Timothy Pappas, managing partner at executive-search firm Pappas Delaney, LLC, Greenfield, Wis., tells the story of presenting a candidate to a client. "The candidate proceeded to get tipsy at the interview," Pappas recalls. "They were going to hire him, but as the evening wore on, his mouth became looser and less professional—he had lost his edge. Even slight amounts of alcohol change your perception. You might feel looser, but you might dull your edge, too," Pappas notes.

The employer could be testing you to see if you will drink. Drinking could signal to the employer a lack of self-control. If the employer's culture seems strongly oriented toward drinking, everyone at the table is having a drink, and they are encouraging you to do the same, you can still finesse your way out of doing so. Cheerfully order water, club soda with a twist, or iced tea, as though those choices were no different from alcohol. Or try a strategy Pamela Harman, lead workers' compensation attorney at Tucker Bower Robin & Merker in Chicago, has used. Harman, who describes herself as petite with a low tolerance for alcohol, pleads that she is still on antibiotics from a mean sinus infection, and the doctor told her not to drink.

Panel interview

A panel interview is one in which you are interviewed by a group of people, usually around a table. Panel interviews can occur at any stage of the interview process, although they are uncommon at the screening stage. They are usually highly structured, with panel members asking the same set of questions in the same order of each candidate, with each panel member asking a specific array of questions. If by chance some panelists don't ask you questions, find another way to connect with every member. Ideally you will have learned ahead of time that you'll be in a panel interview and learned who the panelists will be. You can then research them and personalize your responses. When responding to an individual panelist, make eye contact with that person, but also glance at the other panelists as you respond.

Board of Directors interview

Typically, boards of directors interview only the highest level of executive, usually prospective CEOs. However, as we'll see in Chapter 6, boards sometimes interview other high-level executives. Learn more about how to handle board interviews through the experiences of the case-study subjects and subsequent commentary in Chapter 6.

Presentation interview

The good news about presentation interviews is that you will virtually always know ahead of time if you are expected to deliver a presentation in your interview. To be asked on the spot to give presentation in an interview would be quite unusual.

The other interesting aspect of the presentation interview is that you can sometimes choose to initiate this format yourself, as interviewing expert Eric Kramer recommends. "An effective interview presentation consists of a format that presents the reasons a candidate is the best choice, covers all relevant job requirements, transitions smoothly from topic to topic, and makes a strong finish," Kramer says in an article on Quintessential Careers. Kramer advises developing a set of slides, for which he has determined a winning format.

Remote interview via video

Many organizations are cutting down on the cost of flying out-of-area candidates to interviews by conducting these meetings remotely in formats variously called teleconference, videoconference, or Web conference interviews.

These remote interviews call upon executives to use skills that may be unfamiliar, such as camera presence. Some tips for looking your best on camera include having makeup applied by a professional who specializes in makeup for the camera (even light makeup for men); looking into the camera; avoiding significant movements, fidgeting, and hand gestures that will look exaggerated on camera; and guarding against making any extraneous noises that the microphone might pick up. If you don't have much experience on camera, seek out a career coach knowledgeable in this area. Even a coach who trains individuals for media interviews can be helpful.

Work-assignment/simulation/problem-solving interview

Increasingly, and especially at the senior level, employers require candidates to do more than interview; they also require a hands-on activity. Charles Handler, president and founder of Rocket-Hire.com, calls these activities "a miniature replica of activities that are required on the job." Robinson, for example, gives an assignment, a 30/60/90 Day Performance Plan, when he has narrowed the field to one or two frontrunners. Describing the assignment as "an opportunity to set your agenda for your first three months with us," Robinson asks the finalists to write a 30/60/90-day action plan for what they will do in the role over the first three months. He seeks not a detailed business plan, but "a bulleted list of the accomplishments you'd see as important to make in each of your first three months here."

Another common activity is an inbox simulation in which candidates prioritize and handle various communications that have arrived in their imaginary inboxes, thus demonstrating decision-making, time-management, organization, and prioritization skills. This activity can take from one to several hours. You can learn more about this activity here: *www.elitetraining.co.uk/business_game/In_Box.htm.*

Other activities include the leaderless group discussion, in which a group of candidates discusses a job-related problem, and role-plays. Some experts group case interviews and presentation interviews under the work-assignment/simulation/problem-solving rubric.

Obviously the best preparation for a work-assignment/simulation/problem-solving interview is knowing ahead of time to expect it; here's where researching the type of interview you will undergo is critical. Most employers will tell you to expect this type of interview, but some may spring it on you unexpectedly to see how well you rise to the challenge. If you know a hands-on activity is expected in the interview, learn as much about it as you can. Get a good night's sleep before the activity—it may last several hours. Embrace the activity as an opportunity to show how well you can do the job.

Stress interview

The stress interviewing technique is typically used only for positions in which the candidate will face significant stress on the job. The interviewer wants to evaluate how well the interviewee can handle the pressure. The key to surviving stress interviews is to remain calm, keep a sense of humor, and avoid getting angry or defensive.

The interviewer may try to stress you in one of several ways, such as asking four or five questions in a row, acting rude or sarcastic, disagreeing with you, or simply keeping you waiting for a long period.

Don't take any of these actions personally. Simply stick to your agenda and showcase your skills and accomplishments calmly. Better, try taking back control of the interview by ignoring the stress. Some experts suggest even getting up and walking around the room so that you take control by being the only person standing. If there is a board or flip chart in the room, another option is to get up and draw or diagram parts of your answers.

Most candidates will not encounter stress interviews, but it is important to know they exist, and know how to handle yourself if you are faced with such an interview style.

Overview of content types

Many, if not most, interviewers ask not just one type of question in interviews. That's why its best to familiarize yourself with all question types and prepare yourself to respond to them effectively.

Traditional/screening questions

These types of questions are typically asked early in the interview process, often as part of a phone interview, to "pre-qualify" you for your first or second face-to-face interview. Sometimes a human resources professional will conduct this type of interview. Most traditional and screening questions are easy to prepare for because they appear on countless lists of frequently asked job interview questions available on the Internet. These will usually be broad-based questions such as, "why do you want to work for this company?" and "tell me about your strengths and weaknesses." Given the typically preliminary or screening nature of these questions, your interviewing success is often based on the ability of the candidate to communicate rather than on the content of their answers. Employers are looking for the answer to three questions:

1. Does the candidate have the skills and abilities to perform the job?

2. Does the candidate possess the enthusiasm and work ethic that the employer expects?

3. Will the candidate be a team player and fit into the organization?

Another approach interviewers sometimes take in screening interviews is to use the candidate's resume to guide the interview (hence the traditional/screening type of question is sometimes called the "resume question"). The interviewer will take the candidate through his or her resume and ask questions about each item. The interviewer may ask for clarification about or even substantiation of claims made in the resume. He or she could even ask questions like, "What did you do in this job?" when the answer is right on the resume. Here, the interviewer may be looking for consistency between what you articulate verbally and what you've said on paper. Obviously, you will want to know your resume well before interviewing.

An important aspect of screening that the interviewer may target with this type of interview questioning is compensation. The employer will likely want to screen out candidates that the organization perceives as out of its price range, or less often, whose previous compensation is so low that the employer does not view the applicant as being at the appropriate level for the job.

See strategies for and sample answers to traditional and screening questions in Chapter 5.

Behavioral questions

Although behavioral interviewing has been in use since the 1970s, it is sometimes characterized as a "new" form of interviewing. Increasing numbers of employers use behavior-based methods to interview job candidates, so understanding how to excel in this interview environment has become a crucial skill.

The premise behind behavioral interviewing is that the most accurate predictor of future performance is past performance in similar situations. Behavioral interviewing, in fact, is said to be 55 percent predictive of future on-the-job behavior, while traditional interviewing is only 10 percent predictive.

Behavioral-based interviewing is touted as providing a more objective set of facts to make employment decisions than other interviewing methods. Traditional and screening interview questions focus on a general scope of inquiry, such as "Tell me about yourself." The process of behavioral interviewing is much more probing and works very differently.

In a traditional job interview, you can usually get away with telling the interviewer what he or she wants to hear, even if you are fudging a bit on the truth. Even if you are asked situational questions that start out, "How would you handle XYZ situation?" you have minimal accountability. How does the interviewer know, after all, if you would really react in a given situation the way you say you would? In a behavioral interview, however, it's much more difficult to give responses that are untrue to your character. When you start to tell a behavioral story, the behavioral interviewer typically will pick it apart to try to get at the specific behaviors. The interviewer will probe further for more depth or detail such as, "What were you thinking at that point?" or "Tell me more about your meeting with that person," or "Lead me through your decision process." If you've told a story that's anything but totally honest, your response will not hold up through the barrage of probing questions.

Employers use the behavioral interview technique to evaluate a candidate's experiences and behaviors so they can determine the applicant's potential for success. The interviewer identifies job-related experiences, behaviors, knowledge, skills, and abilities that the employer has decided are desirable in a particular position.

The employer then structures pointed questions to elicit detailed responses aimed at determining if the candidate possesses the desired characteristics. See strategies for responding to behavioral questions in Chapter 5.

Case and brainteaser questions

If you interviewed back when you were a business-school undergraduate or new MBA—chances are, you recall the case interview, a very specialized kind of job interview and the primary interviewing technique that management-consulting firms and investment-banking companies use. Increasingly, other types of corporations, such as Microsoft, are using case and brainteaser questions as at least part of the job interviewing process. These questions are not often asked at the executive level, although some of the techniques recommended for responding to them (described in Chapter 5) are helpful in addressing problem-solving questions.

Case interviews are designed to scrutinize the skills that are especially important in management consulting and related fields: quantitative skills, analytical skills, problem-solving ability, communications skills, creativity, flexibility, the ability to think quickly under pressure, listening skills, business acumen, keen insight, interpersonal skills, the ability to synthesize findings, professional demeanor, and powers of persuasion. Types of case questions that may be asked include:

o   Calculation/estimation/guesstimate/numerical/market sizing case
o   Problem case
o   Probing case
o   Business operations case
o   Business strategy case
o   Resume case (case based on a company at which you worked)
o   Brainteaser/logical puzzle/IQ question

If you are facing a case interview, take comfort in knowing that a vast collection of resources is available, both on and off the Internet, to tell you everything you need to know to succeed in a case interview; see Chapter 5, and Appendix A. Perhaps most helpful are the resources provided by companies that conduct case interviews.

Situational questions

In situational interviewing, candidates are asked to respond to a specific hypothetical situation they may face on the job, and some aspects are similar to behavioral interviews. These types of questions are designed to draw out your analytical and problem-solving skills, as well as how you handle problems with short notice and minimal preparation.

Situational interviews are similar to behavioral interviews, except while behavioral questions focus on a past experience, situational questions focus on a hypothetical situation. For example, in a behavioral interview, the interviewer might start a question with, "Tell me about a time you had to deal with..." In a situational interview, the interviewer asks, "How would you handle..." See Chapter 5, for how to handle situational questions.

Industry-specific questions

Beyond the overarching skills and knowledge that any high-level professional needs to perform well, your deep knowledge and expertise of your specific sector and your industry-related technical skills also will come under scrutiny in the interview. These questions will be especially challenging for those seeking to change industries. These questions are often asked in second and subsequent interviews as employers get down to the nitty-gritty of your qualifications. Learn more about strategies for responding to these questions in Chapter 5.

Off-the-wall questions

Off-the-wall questions are also known as "wild card" or "no-right-answer" questions. Occasionally, you'll be asked an interview question that's just downright weird and certainly doesn't seem to have anything to do with the job—for example: "If you were ice cream, what flavor would you be?" Interviewers often ask these oddball questions to see how quickly you can think on your feet and whether you can avoid becoming flustered. Others, unfortunately, ask them because they enjoy seeing interviewees squirm. Still others find amusement in the range of creative—and not-so-creative—responses they receive. Although off-the-wall questions are not often asked at executive and senior levels, Chapter 5 offers strategies for responding.

Illegal and inappropriate questions

Questions that bear no relationship to your ability to carry out the functions of the job are likely inappropriate and may be illegal. These questions often focus on personal situations or characteristics. Employers that ask them may be ignorant of the law or deliberately looking to screen you out based on some type of bias. Chapter 5 looks more closely at the types of questions that are illegal and inappropriate and describes a strategy for responding.

Structured interview

A structured interview, as the name suggests, follows a specific set of questions, and the same set of questions is typically asked of all candidates. Research suggests that structured interviews result in greater validity in the hiring process.

Unstructured interview

An unstructured interview is more like a conversation. No standard set of questions is used, and the interview conversation can vary significantly from candidate to candidate. Robinson contends that most managers conduct interviews that are more like conversations. An interview over a meal, often designed to evaluate how well a candidate fits into the organizational culture, will likely be unstructured.

While some interviewers simply prefer an unstructured, conversational style or believe that this loose approach works for them, an unstructured interview can also raise a red flag that the person using it is simply not a skilled interviewer. In an unstructured interview, you may need to look for opportunities to direct the conversation to important aspects of your qualification that need to be covered. A section in Chapter 6, on handling a poor interviewer, describes strategies for guiding an interview that lacks structure.

Of course, many unstructured interviews are far from negative. Some interviewers have good reasons for not structuring their interviews and conduct them artfully. Rick McDowell, senior recruiter at Staff Resources Inc., in Farmington Hills, Mich., says that much of his questioning is "improvised" based on the information he gets from candidates. "I have learned that it is better to make the candidate as comfortable as possible and then let them talk," McDowell says. "Let them or get them to talk about themselves as much as possible, really try [to] get to know them on a personal level. The more information that you can find out about the candidate's life, the better." McDowell's approach is designed to go beyond prepared responses for typical interview questions. "A person would be surprised at how many candidates can have great answers to general interview questions, but when you really start getting to know them is when the red flags start popping up," he says. Chapter 5 expands on these content types, provides sample questions, and suggests strategies for responding to each type.

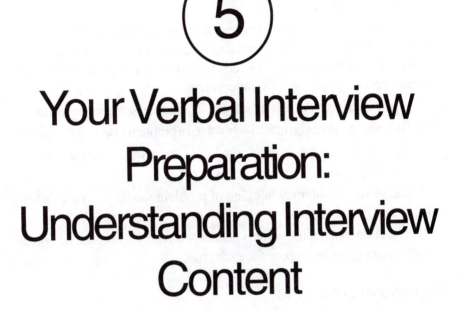

Your Verbal Interview Preparation: Understanding Interview Content

To truly prepare for executive interviews, know what kinds of questions to expect and take inspiration from the responses to those questions that have helped others succeed in top-level interviews. Far more important is the ability to quickly analyze each question to understand what the interviewer is driving at by asking it and choose the best strategy for responding. Think of each interview question as an opportunity to showcase at least one accomplishment or strength. Every response should build momentum toward convincing the interviewer that you deserve to advance to the next level, whether that level is another round of interviews or a job offer.

This chapter expands on main content genres mentioned in Chapter 4 and tells how to prepare for these content types. It then breaks questions down into subject areas, explains what the interviewer is getting at with the questions in each area, provides a strategy for responses to questions in each area, lists sample interview questions for each area, and provides a sample response in each subject area.

Approaching interview-question content genres

Interview-question content genres relate to the way questions are asked. Interviewers have the option of targeting the same subject matter in a variety of ways. It would be possible to ask the same question using any of the genres. Let's take problem-solving as a subject area:

Are you an effective problem-solver?: Traditional screening question

Tell me about a time you effectively solved a problem.: Behavioral question

How would you solve this problem?_____: Situational question

Solve this problem:_____: Case question

If you were a problem, what kind of problem would you be?: Off-the-wall question

This section looks at the various genres—ways questions can be asked—and offers strategies to prepare for each type.

Behavioral questions

As we saw in Chapter 4, behavioral questions are based on the premise that past behavior is the best predictor of future behavior. Recall that behavioral questions (often not even framed as a question) typically start out: "Tell me about a time..." or "Describe a situation..." Example questions are: "Tell me about a time where you confronted an unexpected problem," "Describe an experience when you failed to achieve a goal," and "Give me a specific example of a time when you managed several projects at once."

Equip yourself to answer the questions thoroughly. Obviously, you can prepare better for this type of interview if you know which skills the employer has predetermined to be necessary for the job you seek. Researching the company, studying the job description, and talking to people who work there will enable you to zero in on the kinds of behaviors the company wants. In the interview, your response must be specific and detailed. Candidates who tell the interviewer about particular situations that relate to each question will be far more successful than those who respond in general terms.

Ideally, briefly describe the situation, the specific action you took to have an effect on the situation, and the positive result or outcome. It's also helpful to think of your responses as stories. Frame each example as a three-step story, usually called a S-A-R, P-A-R, or C-A-R statement: 1. situation (or problem, challenge), 2. action, 3. result/outcome. Become an engaging storyteller in your interviews, but be careful not to ramble.

It's difficult to prepare for a behavior-based interview because of the huge number and variety of behavioral questions you might be asked. The best way to prepare is to arm yourself with a small arsenal of example stories that you can adapt to many behavioral questions. Despite myriad possible behavioral questions, you can get some idea of what to expect by looking at Websites that feature behavioral questions (see Appendix B for some of these sites), as well as the questions in this chapter that begin with phrases such as "Describe a time..." and "Tell me about a situation..." Knowing what kinds of questions might be asked will help you prepare an effective selection of examples.

At the executive and senior level, interviewers will expect most of your examples to spring from your professional experience, but it's acceptable to draw a few responses from such activities as volunteer work and community service. Wherever possible, quantify your results. At the executive level, interviewers especially want to hear these outcome metrics.

Remember that many behavioral questions endeavor to probe the way you responded to negative situations; you'll need to have examples of negative experiences ready, but try to choose negative experiences that you made the best of or—better yet, those who had positive outcomes or that you learned from.

Here's an effective way to prepare for behavior-based interviews:

o   Identify up to 20 examples from your past experience in which you demonstrated top behaviors and skills that your research has indicated that the targeted employer seeks. Think in terms of examples that will exploit your top selling points.

o   Half your examples should be totally positive, such as achieving accomplishments or meeting goals.

o   The other half should be situations that started out negatively but either ended positively or you made the best of (or learned from) the outcome.

- o Vary your examples; don't take them all from just one area of your career.

- o Use fairly recent examples—within the last year is best. Some employers, in fact, specify that candidates give examples of behaviors demonstrated within the last year.

- o Describe examples in story form using a P-A-R/S-A-R/C-A-R structure.

- o Write your example stories down and give them titles. Though you don't want to use these written versions as scripts or memorize your responses, you'll find that writing them helps organize and crystallize them in your mind. Giving them titles will help you recall them from your memory bank more easily.

To cram for a behavioral interview right before you're interviewed, review your resume. Seeing your achievements in print will jog your memory.

In the interview, listen carefully to each question, and pull an example out of your bag of tricks that provides an appropriate description of how you demonstrated the desired behavior. With practice, you can learn to tailor a relatively small set of examples to respond to a diverse range of behavioral questions. Expect interviewers to pose several follow-up questions and probe for details that explore all aspects of a given situation or experience. Some of the sample questions beginning on page 93 are accompanied by probing follow-ups; see especially the question submitted by Todd Rogers on page 104.

Once you've snagged the job, keep a record of achievements and accomplishments so you'll be ready with more great examples the next time you go on a behavior-based interview.

Situational questions

As we saw in Chapter 4, situational interview questions are similar to behavioral questions. In a behavioral interview, the interviewer focuses on past behavior and begins a question with a phrase like, "Tell me about a time you had to deal with..." In a situational interview, the interviewer focuses on hypothetical behavior and asks, "How *would* you handle..."

As with behavioral-interview preparation, the key to success in situational interviews is to review your past work experiences and recall the steps you took to resolve problems and make corrections. Develop short stories of these past experiences to incorporate into responses that show your experience in handling similar situations.

Here's one way an interviewer might ask a candidate for a sales director position: "How would you handle an angry customer who was promised delivery of the product on a certain date, but because of manufacturing delays, the company was not able to deliver on a timely basis? The customer is demanding some kind of compensation for the unexpected delay."

Or, for a management position, a candidate might be asked: "How do you handle a disgruntled employee in your department who has made a habit of arriving late to work and causing minor disruptions during the day, as well as a declining morale among the rest of the staff?"

Respond to these questions the same way you would to behavioral questions. "I would handle the angry customer the same way I did in my current job...[tell story about successfully resolving an angry-customer situation]." And: "I would handle the disgruntled employee the same way I handled a similar situation at ABC Corporation...[tell story about successfully handling disruptive employee and low morale]."

Case and brainteaser questions

As we saw in Chapter 4, case and brainteaser questions are essentially problem-solving exercises that focus on the process the interviewee uses to solve the problem. The correct solution is secondary. Case questions are not asked often at the senior and executive level, but Tony Lamb, a systems analyst who responded to survey questions for this book, recalled one an interviewer asked him: "I want a cow. Sell me a pig." Lamb related that he and his interviewer spent a lot of time on this question. "I asked him why he wanted the cow, and he kept saying he just wanted one," he remembered. Lamb correctly emphasized his problem-solving process in his response: "My point was to identify his requirements and determine if we could get the same results in a smaller and cheaper package—the pig," he said, adding, "In retrospect, a funnier answer, although not a better one, would have been 'I'm all out of cows...how about this pig?'"

Josh Chernin, general manager at Web Industries, Marlborough, Mass., says he loves to ask brainteaser questions like "'How many piano tuners are there in Chicago?' just to see what [candidates' reaction are] and whether they have the analytical skills to come up with a plausible answer."

While case questions aren't common at the executive level, the techniques for approaching them are applicable to typical executive-interview questions that require problem-solving. Experts agree on these fine points:

- o Practice before undergoing a case interview. Some companies that use case interviews provide good information on their Websites. Boston Consulting Group, for example, provides interactive cases you can work through for practice, as well as additional cases you can rehearse at *www.bcg.com/careers/ interview_prep/practice_case/practice_cases.html.* Harvard Business School produces numerous case studies that you can use for practice.

- o Listen carefully to the question. Paraphrase it back to the interviewer to ensure your understanding. You may also want to take notes; in most cases the interviewer will allow you to do so. Vault.com suggests bringing not only a pad of paper but also a pad of graph paper in case you want to create a graph as part of your conclusion.

- o Remember that rarely is there one "right" answer for analyzing a case. Your process for reaching your conclusions is equally important to the interviewer as is the conclusion itself. In fact, the interviewer wants to observe as much of that process as possible, so it's important—once you've taken the time to gather your thoughts—to "think out loud" as you're working through the case.

- o Don't be afraid to ask questions. The case interview is meant to be interactive, with lots of back and forth between you and the interviewer. Questions are expected, especially because the information provided about the case may be incomplete. The interviewer will be looking at your resourcefulness in collecting information.

- o Construct a logical framework with which to explore the critical issues of the case. Examples include Porter's Five Forces, the SWOT analysis, Value Chain Analysis, and the marketing mix. You can also draw on applicable situations you've encountered in your business career. Make sure your conclusion is grounded in action, not just theory. Be able to explain and defend your reasoning. For a quick refresher on these terms, see *www.quickmba.com/*.

o Prioritize the issues and objectives. Don't get bogged down trying to deal with every aspect of the case. As you ask questions, try to pick up clues as to which issues are most important.

Off-the-wall questions

Like case questions, off-the-wall questions aren't often asked at the senior and executive levels. Here's one that an interviewer asked Guy Tweedale that centered around Blackpool Rock, a type of candy popular in the UK that has a word running through its center: "If you were a stick of Blackpool Rock, and I cut you across the middle, what word would I see that describes what you do?" Tweedale, who is now senior vice president and general manager for Europe, the Middle East, and Africa at Jacada in London, was interviewing for a position as a vice president of marketing, "and the guy wanted to know if I was a product-marketing type or marketing-communication type," Tweedale recalls. "The end result was a deep discussion about how one can be both with ease," he said.

Don't let an off-the-wall question rattle you. Take a moment to gather your thoughts and respond the best way you can. There is rarely a wrong answer to this type of question, but quick-thinking candidates can turn the response into an opportunity to impress the employer. A response that one interviewee gave me has always stuck in my head as being a standout answer. The question was: "If you were a superhero, what would be your super powers, and why?" His response: "I would prefer to be a superhero like Batman, who doesn't have superpowers per se, but who relies on his intelligence and use of the right tools to get the job done."

Illegal and inappropriate questions

It's illegal to ask about age, national origin, marital and family status, religious affiliation, disabilities, medical history, arrest records, credit history, and childcare arrangements, but employers still do—or come up with subtle ways to get around the illegality. Other questions are not illegal, but inappropriate. Early in my career, I was routinely asked my husband's occupation. The underlying concern was that he was in a career that might require frequent relocation, and I would not be able to stay long with the organization.

It's best to address the concern behind the question rather than the question itself. If you are asked, for example, what your childcare arrangements are, you can say: "Perhaps you are concerned that I will miss work if my childcare arrangements are not reliable. I can assure you that won't happen." You can also say something like: "There is nothing about my personal status that would get in the way of my doing a great job for your company." While it may also be tempting to point out the illegality of the question, doing so likely won't endear you to the interviewer.

You can also answer honestly if you are certain that doing so will not open you up to the employer's discrimination or prejudice (after all, an employer who would ask an illegal question might very well discriminate). For example, it's legal to ask about organizations you belong to that are relevant to the job you're interviewing for, but an employer cannot ask an open-ended question about all the organizations and social clubs of which you are a member. If an employer did that, and you honestly answered that you belong to the Rotary Club, that response would be unlikely to hurt your chances at getting the offer.

Yes-or-no questions and industry-specific questions

Yes-or-no questions and industry-specific questions deserve special mention because they are hybrids of content genres and content subject areas.

Yes-or-no questions are typical in screening interviews but can be asked at any interview phase and on any interview subject area. They are not common at the executive level because interviewers at this level usually ask questions that solicit greater depth; on the other hand, the interviewer may be testing you to see if you will respond with a simple yes or no, or whether you will give a more detailed response. Always respond to a yes-or-no question with more than a one-word answer. A typical yes-or-no question is, "Are you a team player?" A good response would start off, "Yes, and let me give you an example of how I've demonstrated that quality..."

Industry-specific questions are hybrids because they can be asked in any of the content genres (behavioral, situational, etc.). Obviously, they are questions that focus on the candidate's knowledge and skills related to a particular industry. More about industry-specific questions appears later in this chapter.

Approaching interview-question subject areas: employer motivation, response strategies, sample questions, and responses

While the foregoing content genres represent ways of asking questions, the next section examines the most common subject areas for interview questions. Hiring experts tend to develop shortlists of the executive attributes that they believe interviews need to reveal; these attributes then become the basis for subject areas from which interview questions are drawn. Adam Robinson, founder and CEO of the Ionix Hiring Systems (whose recommended set of interview questions is integrated into the questions in this section), targets quality of work, quantity of work, job knowledge and technical application, organization and planning, judgment and decision-making, self-improvement and initiative, innovation and creativity, interpersonal skills, written and oral communication, and teamwork.

Social networking strategist David Nour focuses on candidates' ability to identify their current strengths as well as the gaps in their current abilities, and where they would like to be in the future; performance under pressure; completion of initiatives that clearly demonstrate core strengths and capabilities; supporting colleagues by taking a genuine interest in their key initiatives and helping them to achieve quantifiable results; written and oral communications skills; the ability to confront others or issues with respect, and problem-solve with decisiveness; a high degree of influence that reinforces the ability of proactively engaging others and getting things done; the ability to take on difficult projects and offer value-based counsel; and the ability to succinctly define long-term goals and objectives with a road map of how current and future activities will help in obtaining those goals. The ability "to lead cross-functional teams and deal with complex organizational structures—board of directors, matrix environment, and global markets"—is what Brian Sekandi, principal search consultant, Gilmore Partners, Canada, looks for.

The subject areas in this section are synthesized from these and other experts. The questions in each subject area can fall into virtually any of the content genres presented in the previous section; for example, a question in a given subject area could be asked as a behavioral question, a situational question, or even a case/brainteaser or off-the-wall question. Thus, among the sample questions for each subject area, you will find a mix of content genres. As mentioned in Chapter 2, Glassdoor.com (*www.glassdoor.com/Interview/ index.htm*) is an excellent resource because users submit actual questions from the interviews they've participated in, so you can get a feel for questions that interviewers are currently asking.

* Denotes a question contributed by Adam Robinson, who has, over the course of more than 2,500 interviews, developed a comprehensive, competency-based interview guide to assess talent. His questioning techniques, described from the hiring decision-maker's perspective at http:// betterhiringtoday.com/, offer unusual insight into the interviewer's mindset. Questions are reprinted with permission.

Icebreaker/screening/sell-yourself questions

Interviewer motivation for asking: These questions are typically asked early in the interview process, such as in a phone interview or screening interview conducted by human resources, as well as early in an individual interview.

The interviewer's motivation in many cases is to decide whether to move you forward in the interview process; some of these questions are designed to screen you out if you don't fit the criteria for the responses the employer seeks. Typical screening questions include those focusing on your willingness to relocate or travel. If those are job requirements, and you're not willing to consider moving or traveling, you would be screened out. Of course, you won't find yourself in that position if you've done your research because you will already know that the job requires relocation or travel, and you would not be in the interview if you weren't willing.

Another motivation is to break the ice, put you at ease (that's the theory, though questions like, "Tell me about yourself" can be nerve-wracking), and help the interviewer learn more about you. These questions also challenge you to explain why you are here—why are you interviewing for this job. That challenge is an opportunity to sell yourself.

Strategy for response: Because some of these questions are asked so frequently, here are strategies for those asked most often:

The "Tell Me about Yourself" question. This question, of course, is not a question at all, but a request for a command performance. It's the most commonly asked interview question, yet it frequently still rattles interviewees. The trick is to make your response a succinct summary of information that is specifically targeted to the job you're interviewing for; in other words, you will respond to this question differently for each job you interview for. You want to present yourself so that the interviewer will think the job description for this position was written with your background—and no other candidate's—in mind. The interviewer is really giving you an opportunity to sell yourself and show you understand the organization's needs and priorities; he or she is not looking for your autobiography or highlights of your personal life unless aspects of it are relevant to the job you're interviewing for.

The "Weakness" Question. The conventional wisdom about responding to "What are your weaknesses?" used to be that the candidate should spin a weakness into a strength. For example: "I'm a perfectionist and don't believe anyone can do the job as well as I can, so I sometimes have a hard time delegating." That type of response has, however, worn out its welcome with interviewers. Other approaches include offering a weakness that is inconsequential to the job (such as being a poor speller and relying on spellcheck) or denying that you have any weaknesses that would stand in the way of your performing the job effectively. The former approach may work but could be seen as shallow, while the latter lacks credibility. After all, everyone has a weakness.

An approach that seems to work well is to talk about an area that was once a weakness but that you have worked to improve. Here's how you could frame the perfectionist example above in terms of professional growth: "I tend to be a perfectionist who has had trouble delegating tasks to others, but I've come to see that teamwork and capitalizing on everyone's strengths is a much more effective way to get the job done than trying to do it all myself."

The "Why should we hire you?" question. The unspoken part of this question is: "Why should we hire you [above all the other candidates]?" This is your chance to shine, to truly deliver a sales pitch for yourself. Use your Unique Selling Proposition (an advertising term for the one thing that distinguishes you, as a "product" from other candidates) to describe what sets you apart from others vying for the same job. The employer will make a significant investment in hiring and training you, so assure the interviewer that this investment will be justified. For example, you could say: "I sincerely believe that I'm the best person for the job. Like other candidates, I have the ability to do this job. But beyond that ability, I offer an additional quality that makes me the very best person for the job—my drive for excellence. Not just giving lip service to excellence, but putting every part of myself into achieving it. Throughout my career, I have consistently strived to become the very best I can become. [Give an example or two.] The success I've attained in my management positions is the result of possessing the qualities you're looking for in an employee." Then, tell a story that describes an example of applying the relevant qualities in a past job. Finally, be sure to express your strong interest in the position; the employer should hire you because you sincerely want to work there.

Because the questions in the icebreaker/screening/sell yourself category can cover such a wide territory, one very good way to prepare for them and strategize your responses is to search the Internet for frequently asked interview questions. You'll find countless sets of them, though most sets will be quite similar to each other. Here's a strategy that fits virtually all of these questions:

- Identify one to three top selling points that you would like to communicate to the interviewer with each response. Be sure these selling points are relevant to position you're interviewing for (you'll know because of the research you've done).

- Relate each response specifically to the organization at which you're interviewing and the position you're interviewing for. For example, the desired response to the request "describe your ideal job" is that your ideal job is the job you're interviewing for. Describe the elements of the organization and position that perfectly fit your qualifications and attributes. Similarly, the best way answer the question, "What are your strengths?" is to list strengths relevant to the employer and the position.

o   Quantify whenever possible. In your "tell me about yourself" response, for example, use metrics such as percentage by which you've increased revenue or reduced costs, number of projects you've brought in on time and under budget.

Sample questions in this subject area:

o   Tell me about yourself/How would you describe yourself?

o   Please describe your ideal job.

o   What do you want in your next job?

o   Why should we hire you?

o   What separates you from your colleagues? (contributed by Daniel Berger, executive recruiter at Joel Paul & Associates, New York City)

o   Why do you believe you are the best candidate for this position?

o   How will we know we've made the right decision by hiring you?

o   What personal weakness has caused you the greatest difficulty on the job?

o   Why shouldn't we hire you? (This twist on the weakness question was contributed by Colin Brown, president, Search & Employ, Ottawa)

o   *What one area do you really need to work on in your career to become more effective on a day-to-day basis?

o   If you could change something about your [life] [career], what would it be?

o   Do you have a geographic preference?

o   Would it be a problem for you to relocate?

o   How much travel are you willing to do for the job?

o   What two or three things are most important to you in your job?

o   What are your strengths?

o   *Tell me about your greatest strength, and why it will benefit our company.

Sample response for this subject area:

Question: What personal weakness has caused you the greatest difficulty on the job?

Response: I've always had a knack—an instinct—for seeing the big picture. I can review an analysis of a situation and within a short period, develop a strategy that will result in positive return for the company. What's been harder for me, though, is that I was raised in a family with poor people skills, and for many years, when I first started in this business, this inability to talk to colleagues hurt my career. Luckily, when I was working for GE, I found a mentor who showed me the error of my ways and helped me get the training I needed. He flat-out told me that I would never advance beyond middle management unless I learned how to communicate with people. It was an eye-opening experience, and while I still believe my greatest strength is my knack for strategic problem-solving, I can honestly say that I am now quite good at communicating that message in a way that motivates my employees and helps move the company forward at an even more successful rate. (contributed by Randall S. Hansen, PhD, founder and CEO of Quintessential Careers)

Compensation questions

Interviewer motivation for asking: As a screening device, interviewers often ask early in the interview or interview process what salary you are looking for. If you ask for more than the employer is willing to pay (or occasionally, on the flip side, undervalue yourself), the interviewer can eliminate you before spending a lot of time with you.

Strategy for response: For many years, the common advice on salary questions has been to delay responding with specific figures and deflect these questions as long as possible—ideally until after the employer has made an offer. In his book, *Negotiating your Salary; How to Make $1000 a Minute*, author Jack Chapman, arguably the best-known expert on salary negotiations, offers sample evasive statements candidates can use in response to questions like, "What salary are you looking for?" Pamela K. Harman, lead workers' compensation attorney at Tucker Bower Robin & Merker in Chicago, reflects the frustration candidates feel with such tactics: "The responses we were told to use felt fake and coy." Harman notes that, "in a perfect world, the interviewer would signal a range and ask if my expectations fall within it. The company knows its budget; I assume they would not waste interview time with me if they didn't think my resume supported their budgeted target."

The approach that Judy Rosemarin suggests supports this idea that the company knows its budget. Rosemarin, president of Sense-Able Strategies, Inc., New York City, points out that the interviewer is rarely part of the process when salaries are budgeted and that budget guidelines are not usually set in stone. Salary is also only one part of total compensation, Rosemarin notes. "Your first response should be, 'what is this job budgeted for?' If you are pressed back, then offer a range, not a figure, and let the interviewer know that a fuller description of the job would make it easier to talk about compensation."

As a job-seeker, Harman was well acquainted with the dilemma of giving a figure. "If I ask too little, I undervalue myself and signal that my experience may not be sufficient for this job," Harman says. "If I ask too much, I can price myself out of the market." Whether you give a range or a figure, research is the to key avoiding Harman's former dilemma. You must know three things:

1. Your market value, which you can research using the salary-research tools listed in Appendix B.

2. What the employer is likely to pay (including all aspects of the compensation package), which is harder to learn but can be uncovered through company insiders in your network and SEC 10-k reports (for public companies). The salary research tools listed in the Appendix can also help.

3. What your walk-away number is, which is more likely to come into play after the offer and in the negotiation phase, but could be a significant factor earlier if you learn that you and the employer are miles apart on compensation. Do keep in mind, however, that at the executive level, salary is only one component of a comprehensive compensation package.

Chapman's advice to deflect and delay the salary discussion has merit considering that you really have no negotiating power until you have an offer.

The sample response in this section is a good example of an evasive, yet perfectly reasonable, response. The interviewer asks, "What level of compensation would it take to make you happy?" The interviewee gives a response expressing enthusiasm for the employer and the job and confidence that the company compensates fairly—but does not name a figure. Now, at this point, the interviewer could very well say, "Great, but can you give me a number for the salary you're looking for?" If delaying or evading tactics make you uncomfortable the way they did Harman—or if they don't work because you are pressed for a number—your own solid, confident notion of the salary you want and know you are worth (based on extensive research) then go ahead and name that figure or range.

Sample questions in this subject area:

o   Which is more important to you, the job itself or your compensation?

o   What level of compensation would it take to make you happy?

o   Tell me about the salary range you're seeking.

o   Here is the salary range for this position: $_____ to $_____. Would you be comfortable with that range?

o   Why did you not earn a higher salary in your [last job] [most recent job]?

Sample response for this subject area:

Question: What level of compensation would it take to make you happy?

Response: Compensation is important; I think we can all agree on that issue. And I have researched Google enough to know that you value and reward all your employees well. I have no doubt that the compensation for this position exceeds the industry average. But more important than compensation—what would make me really happy—is joining the management team that helps steer the company in new and profitable directions. To me, the keys to happiness in a job are compensation, creativity, and collaboration—all of which are hallmarks of Google. (contributed by Randall S. Hansen, PhD)

Resume/experience/job history questions

Interviewer motivation for asking: These types of questions are also usually asked early in the interview process or interview. The interviewer wants to know about your experience (and by extension, whether your experience qualifies you for the position), and often more importantly, wants to see how well you can articulate what you did. The interviewer may also want to see how well you know your own resume. While lack of familiarity with your resume might seem odd, you could have hired a professional to write your resume, or you may not have revisited the older experience listed on it for years. Asking resume-related questions is a way for the interviewer to learn about your career progression and see if you've exaggerated your accomplishments. The interviewer may have noticed time gaps in your resume and ask you to account for those gaps in the interview. (See advice on how to do so in Chapter 6.)

Questions about your resume and experience are especially significant if you are making a switch from one job function or industry to another.

Strategy for response: Be sure you know your resume! Practice clearly articulating what you did in your jobs. Don't overwhelm the interviewer; focus on the most significant two or three functions of each job, ideally framed as accomplishments. If you are changing industries, be prepared to make a case for the transferability and applicability of your experience and skills to the new industry. (See Chapter 6.)

Sample questions in this subject area:

o   What skills have you acquired from your work experience?

o   What exactly did you do [in your last job] [in each of your jobs]?

o   How much experience do you have with [a particular job function] [a job-related skill] [the product/service the organization purveys] [this industry sector]?

o   Tell me about the promotions you've earned.

o   How many direct reports did you have in your most recent position?

Sample response for this subject area:

Question: How much experience do you have with technology and IT infrastructure?

Response: I have the expertise, the training, and the experience to be the next chief technology officer with Cardinal Health. Let me provide you with just three examples that illustrate my point. First, in my current position with Health Management Associates, I oversee the entire technical staff of 130, managing all aspects of IT—from strategic infrastructure decisions to key vendor selection. Second, in my previous position with Medical Mutual of Ohio, I served as the point person for the entire overhaul of an outdated information system, guiding a team in the implementation of a state-of-the-art system. Third, as all of my previous employers will quickly agree, I am adept at listening to the technology needs of the non-technical staff and translating those needs into IT solutions with the technical staff—in other words, I am fluent in the two most powerful languages of any organization, and I am confident I will bring that excellence and expertise to the boardroom at Cardinal Health. (contributed by Randall S. Hansen, PhD)

Employer comprehension and contribution questions

Interviewer motivation for asking: Quite simply, the interviewer wants to know that you've done your homework. The employer expects you to come into the interview with thorough knowledge of the organization and the position, as detailed in Chapter 2. The interviewer wants you to know the organization well enough so that you also know what you can contribute and perhaps how you can respond to the employer's issues and challenges. The degree to which you've researched the employer shows your level of interest in the job. The interviewer may also ask you about the geographic area in which the organization is located if relocation is part of the job.

Strategy for response: Having done your due diligence and performed extensive research on the employer and the job, showcase that knowledge in your responses. Be prepared to demonstrate not only what you know about the organization, position, and geographic area, but also what you like about them. When asked about the contribution you can bring to the employer, relate one of your accomplishments to a need that your research has told you this organization has. If you are asked about solving a company problem, be sure your research has given you sufficient background about the issue before responding. If it has not, ask the interviewer questions (such as finding out what approaches have been applied to this problem in the past and why they haven't worked) to get sufficient information. Don't assume that a solution that worked in one of your past positions will automatically work for this employer.

Sample questions in this subject area:

o Tell me what you know about our company.

o Why did you decide to seek a position in this company?

o Why are you seeking this position?

o Why do you think you might like to live and work in the community in which our company is located?

o If you were hiring for this position, what qualities would you look for?

o What suggestions do you have for our organization?

o What are your expectations for this position?

o What do you expect to contribute to our organization?

o What changes would you make in the organization?

o What can you tell me about our organization's:

    o Size?

    o Key stakeholders?

    o History?

    o Revenues?

    o Products/services?

    o Mission statement?

    o Most recent media releases?

    o Competitors? News about the competitors?

Sample responses for this subject area:

Question: Why do you think you might like to live and work in the community in which our company is located?

Response: The great thing about Bentonville is that the city is a microcosm of WalMart's strengths, as well as the opportunities and challenges facing the company. Bentonville, like many places across the U.S., has changed dramatically since the time when the first WalMart store opened there. In fact, just in the past 40 years or so, the population has more than quadrupled—going from a rural community of about 5,000 people in the 1970s to more than 20,000 today. While still the county seat, the town has seen the development of upscale neighborhoods and shopping centers. Just like the town, WalMart's growth and expansion over the past 40 years has brought amazing success, but also many new challenges, especially as the traditional markets become saturated and the company expands into new and unchartered territory. Thus, driving around Bentonville and talking with the townspeople will not only be a fun and challenging experience—as any move to a new town is—but I believe the experience can also help foster new strategic ideas for helping WalMart achieve even greater success. (contributed by Randall S. Hansen, PhD)

"Why are you transitioning?" questions

Interviewer motivation for asking: Questions about why you are interested in leaving your current job or why you left the most recent position are exceedingly common in interviews. The interviewer is looking for clues about what you've liked and disliked about your jobs to help determine fit with the prospective position. He or she wants to know what motivates you to leave a job to see if that same motivation might cause you to leave this prospective employer. One intent may be to learn whether you have been terminated. The interviewer will want to understand why you are interested in changing job functions or industries, if that's the case, and may be skeptical about your qualifications to do so.

Strategy for response: Always keep a positive focus when responding to transition questions. Never denigrate a former employer or boss. The best responses feature your desire for increased growth and challenge and your fit with the employer. While you don't want to disparage your previous employer, it's fine to say the employer was not an optimal fit for you, whereas you believe the employer you're interviewing with is an excellent fit—and explain why. For more about responses to questions on both voluntary and involuntary departures from your most recent position, see Chapter 6.

Sample questions in this subject area:

o Why do you want to leave your current job?

o Why did you leave your last job?

o Why are you changing industries/careers?

o Why are you unemployed?

Sample response for this subject area:

Question: Why do you want to leave your current job?

Response: There comes a point in just about any job where you have simply achieved everything you can achieve, your company or division is a market leader, and you seek out new challenges because you fear complacency. My current situation at Merck is similar to the situation at General Electric right before Jack Welch stepped down in that we have a very strong CEO who has been grooming three of his top executives to replace him. Unfortunately, only one of us will get the position—and frankly, I am too good at my profession to simply keep doing my job and biding my time—waiting to see if I am the one chosen as his successor. Instead, I am seeking a new challenge to further sharpen and utilize my key mix of talents. I am ready to take the reins of King Pharmaceuticals. I understand your business model of offering the best qualities of a big and small company in one fully integrated pharmaceutical company. My experience, skills, and education position me perfectly to lead a company that develops, manufactures, and markets therapies and technologies primarily in specialty-driven markets, including neuroscience, hospital, and acute-care medicines. (contributed by Randall S. Hansen, PhD)

Success questions

Interviewer motivation for asking: The interviewer seeks to discover how you see success. How well do you understand what makes you successful, how you measure success, and what you need to succeed?

Strategy for response: Success questions provide an excellent opportunity to match your selling points with the requirements of the position you're interviewing for. Your research should have told you the criteria that will contribute to success in this position and with this employer, as well as how the employer measures success. Align those criteria with what you have to offer.

Also be sure you have strong self-knowledge of your own success; if not, consider working with an executive or career coach to refine your understanding.

Sample questions in this subject area:

o   What do you think it takes to succeed in this career?

o   How do you determine or evaluate success?

o   Do you have the qualifications and personal characteristics necessary for success in your chosen career?

o   What quality or attribute do you feel will most contribute to your career success?

o   How would you define "success" for someone in your chosen career?

o   What qualifications do you have that will make you successful in this company?

o   *Describe to me the specific things you know and have experience with that enable you to succeed in your job.

o   In what kind of work environment can you be most successful?

o   What will it take for you to advance to the next level of success in your career?

o   What makes you think you will succeed [in this job] [with this organization]?

o   To what extent have you attained success in adapting to a wide variety of people, situations, and environments?

Sample response for this subject area:

Question: What qualifications do you have that will make you successful in this company?

Response: I have given this question a lot of thought prior to today's interview. When you look at my track record in my previous positions, you see someone who not only provides technical expertise, but who also has a strategic vision and a thirst for continued quality improvements in a cost-effective environment. You also see someone who is a true team player, who realizes her ideas will not always be the ones chosen, and who rallies around and supports the best ideas for moving the company forward.

My years of manufacturing expertise and other qualifications equip me to contribute to modernizing and improving your manufacturing process—ensuring that your production meets or exceeds all company, industry, and customer requirements for cost, quality, and responsiveness. I will manage and lead the production team, continuing my tradition of encouraging full decision-making participation of all employees, as some of the best ideas come from line workers. I will also focus my energies on developing and managing budgeting and budget execution—with a focus on product costs and margins. Finally, I will direct all production control, production process development, quality systems, purchasing, and shipping/receiving activities with a sharp focus on quality, costs, and customer satisfaction.

I also look forward to sharing my ideas—as part of the leadership team—on the strategic direction of the firm, collaborating closely with the leaders of all departments to maximize our profitability and market share while guaranteeing we hold true to our values and build the foundation for our future growth. In these ways, I am confident I will succeed in this company. (contributed by Randall S. Hansen, PhD)

Accomplishment questions

Interviewer motivation for asking: Accomplishments are the meat of any interview because accomplishments yield results. Employers, especially at the executive level, know that a candidate who achieved results for a previous employer is capable of attaining results for the next employer. Accomplishments are so important in the interview that most of your interview responses should include accomplishments—even when you are not asked directly about them.

Strategy for response: Focus on accomplishments that are relevant to the employer and job you are targeting with your interview. The same formula that works for behavioral-interview responses—Situation (or Problem, Challenge)-Action-Result—is an excellent framework for accomplishment stories. To brainstorm accomplishments and ensure you have plenty to provide in interviews, you can use the Accomplishments Worksheet at *www.quintcareers.com/accomplishments_worksheet.html*. Quantify your results as much as possible.

Sample questions in this subject area:

o Give me an example of one of your successful accomplishments.

o What has been your most rewarding accomplishment?

o *Over the course of your career, what role has quality played in your overall performance?

o Which accomplishments especially make you stand out?

o *What have you done in your last/present position to increase your organization's top-line revenues?

o Describe some projects or ideas (not necessarily your own) that were implemented, or carried out successfully primarily because of your efforts.

o What is it about your [life] [career] that makes you most proud?

o How do you do your job better than anyone else could?

o To what extent did you meet or exceed expectations of you in your most recent job?

o Describe the most significant project [in your career] [in your most recent position] [in each of your positions].

o When you look back on your career, walk me through the first thing that comes to mind with respect to your most challenging and successful project. What were the contextual circumstances? What were the challenges? What was your initial thought about the problem/challenge/project? What was your role? What was the outcome? What would you do differently if you were confronted with it now? (contributed by professional recruiter Todd Rogers, Indianapolis, Ind.)

Sample response for this subject area:

Question: How do you do your job better than anyone else could?

Response: Anyone can say they do a better job than others—and at this level, I certainly hope there is at least some truth in that belief. But rather than simply saying, yes, I can transform the marketing functions of this company better than anyone else can, let me give you an example of why I am confident I can do a better job than any other candidate.

As the marketing director for Hansen Beverage Company, I built on the founding family's early—but regional—successes with high-quality, all-natural beverages and leveraged the marketplace by introducing new products and expanding distribution nationally. Within just a few years, I transformed this regional and rather small company into the leader in the natural alternative soda and energy-drink markets. I accomplished this transformation—supported by an amazing team—by understanding our core consumer base. I carefully analyzed changing consumer preferences and identified strategic opportunities. We also outwitted our competition while spending much less in marketing and advertising costs. For example, our Monster Energy drink is one of the most popular products in its category, yet we do very little advertising for the brand—relying more on a carefully crafted mix of powerful word-of-mouth and strategic sponsorship agreements. We also encourage our customers to comment about the brand and offer suggestions—and from these conversations, we have added several flavors that quickly became top sellers.

I bring to the table experience and expertise in all aspects of marketing, from branding and advertising, to customer relationship management, to pricing and packaging. My strengths lie in understanding a brand's core consumers and strengthening existing brands while developing new brands that exploit an opportunity in the marketplace. I thrive in a competitive environment where my marketing initiatives take share away from other brands—all while focusing on existing and emerging marketing strategies that are both efficient and cost-effective. (contributed by Randall S. Hansen, PhD)

Leadership and vision questions

Interviewer motivation for asking: The interviewer wants to get at how you see yourself as a leader, as well as how you have viewed and interacted with other leaders in your background. You are expected to possess a solid concept of the qualities that make an effective leader and how a leader interacts with direct reports.

Strategy for response: Have a strong understanding of your leadership style and the characteristics that make you an effective leader. Be prepared to articulate, with examples, how you influence, motivate, recognize, coordinate, and manage members of your team. Familiarize yourself with leaders of the organization at which you are interviewing, and favorably compare aspects of their leadership abilities with your own. You could also do the same with well-known, highly respected leaders. Be sure not to be negative about past bosses. The interviewer may ask probing questions to see if you will fall into the trap of disparaging a former boss. If you are pushed to talk about a "bad boss," focus on differences in style and give the boss the benefit of the doubt. See, for example, the sample response to a leadership question in this section.

Sample questions in this subject area:

- Describe the characteristics of a successful leader.
- Describe the ideal boss.
- Describe a boss you've had who was not ideal.
- Describe the optimal relationship between leader and subordinate.
- What has been your most challenging leadership dilemma?
- Have you ever had difficulty with someone to whom you reported? How did you resolve the conflict?
- How would you describe your leadership skills?
- How would you characterize your leadership style?
- Give an example of how you've motivated others to excel.
- *Do you consider yourself to be a natural leader of people?
- *When was the last time that someone at work asked you for help? (Are you approachable as a leader?)
- *Describe the person you currently report to or most recently reported to.
- *How does/did the person you report to stay up-to-date on what you're doing?
- *What's your definition of micromanagement?
- *Who's the best boss you've ever had?
- *Who's the worst boss you've ever had?
- In a leadership role, have you ever had to discipline or counsel an employee or group member? What was the nature of the discipline? What steps did you take? How did that make you feel? How did you prepare yourself?

o Give me a specific example of a time when a subordinate criticized your work in front of others. How did you respond? How has that event shaped the way you lead?

o When directing a complex project, how do you coordinate the efforts of team members to achieve results?

o Describe your progressive track record with complex projects. After leading one, have you been selected to lead increasingly large and complex projects?

o Describe a time when you have influenced someone to whom you reported to approve a project.

o Describe a project you led that had a high level of risk or failure or required an unusual level of resources.

o How do you influence people who are not direct reports, such as directors at your level in other departments?

o How have you recognized the performance of subordinates or coworkers?

o What kinds of things have you done to develop your direct reports?

o How have you differed from those you reported to in evaluating your performance? How did you handle the situation?

o What kind of boss do you work best for? Provide examples.

o Give me a specific example of something you did that helped build enthusiasm in others.

o Describe a time when you put your needs aside to help a colleague understand a project. How did you assist him or her? What was the result?

o Describe a situation when you had a positive influence on the actions of others.

o Provide an example of exerting influence and proactively engaging others to get things done.

o Would you challenge your boss if you were certain he or she was wrong and was about to make big mistake?

- Give an example of how you've supported a colleague by taking a genuine interest in his or her key initiatives and helping him or her to achieve quantifiable results.
- How would you handle a dispute with your boss if your boss finally overruled you? (contributed by Josh Chernin, general manager at Web Industries)

Sample response for this subject area:

Question: How would you handle a dispute with your boss if your boss finally overruled you?

Response: There's no point in pretending that people don't have professional disagreements, so I wouldn't even try to deny that in public. My answer to my direct reports would be that it's not a secret that my boss and I disagree on this issue, but I've had my opportunity to say what I want, and he has asked me to follow this direction. I have enough respect for my boss that I will do that, and I'm asking you to as well. (contributed by Josh Chernin)

Future and goal questions

Interviewer motivation for asking: The interviewer wants to determine if you are goal-oriented and how you go about achieving your goals. He or she also wants to get at how you see your future with the prospective employer. Are you planning to stick around for a while?

Strategy for response: When answering questions about future plans, strive for a delicate mix of honesty, ambition, and your desire to be working at this company long-term. Obviously, you want to avoid responses such as, "I want to start my own business" or "I plan to run for Congress," which suggest that you don't plan to stay with the company.

Your response could be: "I'm here to let you know that I am the best person for the job because ...[list relevant skills and bottom-line results that track to the employer's needs]. If in the future you feel I would be a candidate for a higher level position, I know I wouldn't be passed up."

OR: "I hope to stay at the company and expect that in five years, I'll make significant contributions to the organization."

OR: "I would like to become the very best _____ your company has."

And then there's my personal favorite, which I heard secondhand. The interviewer's question was, "Where do you see yourself in five years?" The response: "Celebrating the five-year anniversary of your asking me this question!" While the response likely made the interviewer laugh, it's probably not the best answer.

Because you will probably be asked questions about your goals, be sure you know what your goals are and can articulate them clearly. Be prepared to give examples and tell stories of achieving your goals. When asked about future goals, be sure to integrate the organization you're interviewing for into those goals using the preceding strategy for future questions.

Sample questions in this subject area:

o What specific goals, including those related to your career, have you established for your life?

o What specific goals have you established for your career? What will it take to attain your goals, and what steps have you taken toward attaining them?

o Would you describe yourself as goal-driven?

o Describe what you've accomplished toward reaching a recent goal for yourself.

o What short-term goals and objectives have you established for yourself?

o Can you describe your long-range goals and objectives?

o How does this job align with your long-range goals and objectives?

o How do you see your current and future activities helping you to obtain your goals?

o What do you expect to be doing in five years?

o What do you see yourself doing in 10 years?

o Give me an example of an important goal that you had set in the past and tell me about your success in reaching it.

o Give an example of when you took a risk to achieve a goal. What was the outcome?

o How long are you likely to stay with our organization?

Sample response for this subject area:

Question: Give me an example of an important goal that you had set in the past and tell me about your success in reaching it.

Response: When I was hired as vice president for training for a very large accounting firm, top management told me the company was experiencing a systemic problem with decision-making. Decisions were being made based on "the way we've always done it" rather than strategic, big-picture approaches that looked at the long view. I made it my goal to—within a year—change the way decisions were made and save the company a bundle of money wasted through ineffective decision-making. I sought facilitator training for me and my sharpest deputy. We then initiated a series of workshops for managers in which we stressed teamwork, creative problem-solving, and planning. We taught managers to look for and analyze the root causes of problems, as well as how to anticipate the issues that might crop up after implementing new decisions. I set up a program to recognize and reward instances of the new decision-making process that yielded bottom-line results. I also developed an offsite retreat for the senior leadership team to apply the new techniques to work through decision-making simulations based on real situations in the company. At the end of the year, I had exceeded my goal. The new decision-making process was much clearer and more strategic. I calculated that the process saved the firm $65 million that first year and would save hundreds of millions over the next decade.

Innovation/creativity/improvement questions

Interviewer motivation for asking: More than lower-level employees, people at the senior and executive levels are expected to be creative, innovative, and with a track record of leaving organizations better than they found them.

Strategy for response: Here is where tracking your accomplishments is especially important. Brainstorm job activities that not only were accomplishments but also represent innovation, and show how you have improved operations for previous employers.

Sample questions in this subject area:

o   Which is more important: creativity or efficiency? Why?

o   *Do you consider yourself a creative person?

- o *Describe a time when you created a new way of doing things at work.
- o *Are you more of a detail-oriented person or a big-picture person?
- o What techniques have you found to make a job easier or more rewarding or to make yourself more effective?
- o What has been your most creative achievement?
- o What is the most significant contribution you made to the company during a past job?
- o Tell me about a time when you came up with an innovative solution to a challenge your company/organization was facing. What was the challenge? What role did others play?
- o How have you helped a current employer:
  - o Cut costs?
  - o Generate revenue?
  - o Increase efficiency?

Sample response for this subject area:

Question: What has been your most creative achievement?

Response: When I took over as CEO of the Snicky Snax Company, growth had come to a virtual halt, and performance was stagnating. The snack-food products had once been the leaders in the market. But when I arrived, the snacks were thought of as being targeted at grade-school kids, while competitors were seen as hipper and more desirable to preteens and teens with discretionary money to spend. Distribution channels were very narrow and limited. The staff was conservative and set in its ways. The few people who injected creativity into marketing the products were scorned, especially by the former CEO.

When I came in, I immediately developed an action plan that introduced the idea of change and a new spirit of creativity—gradually so the conservative staff could get used to the new ways. I gathered a task force to conduct a competitive analysis to see where Snicky Snax was vulnerable. I held a retreat where teams could brainstorm creative ideas. To honor the roots of the company that the staff so respected and clung to, I used the Appreciative Inquiry technique, which asks employees to look at what's working in the organization and ask how we can do more of it. I created an atmosphere in which creativity was encouraged and rewarded. I brought back to the company one of the innovative folks who had quit in frustration. I communicated a vision of a growing company that energized and empowered its employees. In the Appreciative Inquiry exercise, we noted that teens and preteens had fond, nostalgic feelings about our market leader, Snicky Chips, but tended to abandon them because they felt they were "kids' stuff." So we hit on the idea of extending the brand to a hipper, teen-targeted line with more sophisticated packaging and bolder flavors. I was proud to be the one who came up with the tagline: "Snicky Chips: All Grown Up." We repositioned the brand and opened up the distribution channels to target teens and preteens. The new line was a runaway smash hit. Perhaps even more importantly, creativity began to flourish at Snicky Snax.

Initiative/self-motivation/learning questions

Interviewer motivation for asking: High-level professionals are self-starters. They are highly motivated and tend to continue to learn and apply their learning. "Top professionals are self-motivated to learn," Robinson says.

They don't sit around and wait to be told what to do; they take the initiative. The interviewer wants to know how you fit that profile. He or she also wants to know what drives you, where your passion is, and how you stay up to date on information in your field.

Strategy for response: Be prepared to talk passionately about your career and why you chose it, especially as it relates to the prospective employer. Have stories ready to illustrate your initiative and self-motivation. Show that you seek and enjoy continuous learning and self-improvement and that you are current with your knowledge of your field.

Sample questions in this subject area:
- What influenced you to choose this career?
- What motivates you to put forth your greatest effort?
- Why did you decide to seek a position in this field?
- Why did you choose your last position? What attracted you?
- What have been the pros and cons of your most recent job?

o In what ways will your next job fulfill you in ways your current/most recent one has not?

o What would be the most de-motivating job you could imagine?

o What are the most important rewards you expect to gain from your career?

o What have you learned from your experiences outside the workplace?

o What have you accomplished that shows your initiative?

o If there was one area you've always wanted to improve upon, what would that be?

o When you have been made aware of, or have discovered for yourself, a problem in your work performance, what was your course of action?

o What kinds of things have you done on the job that were beyond expectations?

o What sorts of things have you done to become better qualified for your career?

o *What standards and procedures for delivering work are/were in place in your current/most recent position? (This is an initiative question because, Robinson says, it gets at "whether or not this candidate's accomplishments were a result of following process, or as a result of winging it," in other words, taking initiative).

o *Tell me about the last professional training or education that you pursued or received.

o *What professional organizations related to this job are you involved with?

o What are you most passionate about?

o *How do you stay current with knowledge?

o What types of professional development have you sought out?

o Describe the last time that you undertook a project that demanded a lot of initiative.

o What motivates you to go the extra mile on a project or job?

- What is the most competitive work situation you have experienced? How did you handle it? What was the result?
- What new skills have you developed in the last several years?
- Tell me about a time when you went above and beyond the call of duty to get a job done.
- Give examples of your experiences in a job that were satisfying. Give examples of your experiences that were dissatisfying.
- What techniques do you employ to ensure your knowledge of [the industry] [relevant technology] is current?
- What has been your most significant initiative [in your most recent job] [in your career] [in each of your past jobs]?
- Tell about a recent job experience that you would describe as a real learning experience. What did you learn from the job or experience?
- In one to three words, what is your profession? (Contributed by Daniel Berger, who notes that the question seems simple, "but people say the oddest things sometimes and that gives me a great feel for how the executive views his or her work.")

Sample response for this subject area:

Question: In what ways will your next job fulfill you in ways your current one has not?

Response: In all my previous positions—whether I advanced to the next level through a promotion or a new job—I knew when it was time to move up because the job no longer challenged me, and I was constantly seeking new opportunities to reach my potential. I am at that point now with my current position. I am ready to lead the entire sales force. I am ready for the challenges that I will face in trying to improve sales in all your regions and territories, especially some of your problem areas. I look forward to the challenge of motivating and teaching the sales force, helping them to reach their potential. I have many ideas for motivating, training, and leading the entire sales force to maximize sales and sales revenues. Becoming vice president of sales also brings me into the strategic inner circle, where I will be challenged to excel, bringing forth mission-driven marketing and sales ideas that will help the organization achieve its goals and vision for the future. I have excelled in my current position as regional sales manager, succeeding in obtaining increased sales—above quota—in all the territories I manage. I want to take that success—and the ideas, strategies, and tactics—and put it to work for you as your VP of sales. (contributed by Randall S. Hansen, PhD)

Knowledge application and expertise questions

Interviewer motivation for asking: The interviewer wants to know the scope of your job-related knowledge, as how well you apply knowledge from one sphere to another. The interviewer also seeks to discover not just where your expertise is strong, but how you apply that expertise on the job. You also may be asked about your knowledge of industry-related specific job functions or processes.

Strategy for response: This line of questioning is especially important for industry-changers. You must be poised to convince the interviewer that you can successfully transfer the skills you used in one industry to the industry you seek to enter. Identify the skills most important to the position and industry you seek to enter and be prepared to describe instances in which you've effectively used those skills (see also Chapter 2). Brainstorm your strongest areas of expertise and develop examples of how you apply that expertise professionally.

Sample questions in this subject area:

o *Give me an example of how you use current information about the industry to increase performance in your role.

o Tell me how you have applied knowledge from another job or other area of your life into your most recent position.

o Describe your knowledge of [a specific industry-related job function or process].

o Describe to me how you would apply your knowledge to address this situation: _____.

o Tell me about a time you successfully used [specific knowledge application] to solve a problem you were facing.

o What do you know about _____?

o How would you apply the expertise you've gained in previous positions in the position you're interviewing for?

Sample response for this subject area:

Question: Tell me how you have applied knowledge from another job or other area of your life to your most recent position.

Response: This might sound kind of funny, but it's a true story and one that I actually discuss with new hires—to show them that not everything they need to know about their work comes from the classroom, textbooks, or even past business experience. I am an avid gardener, and have always had a garden wherever I lived. About midway in my career, however, I took a position with Time-Warner in New York. I lived in the city, and thought that might be the end of my gardening until I found there was a community garden a few blocks from my co-op. To my dismay, the garden was in complete shambles. The story goes that the garden was one person's dream, but when he passed away, no one stepped up to keep it going. That's where I entered the picture—a young hotshot manager who thought he could march in there and take charge of the garden. What I learned in those couple of summers was that there was much more to leadership and teamwork than simply having a good plan. You need people to buy into a plan—most often long before the plan is even fully developed. You need to understand people's motives and goals, and most importantly, you need to understand their personalities—understand what makes them tick and how you can use that information to form a cohesive group focused on a common goal. It was a truly enlightening experience for me, and one I still use to this day in working with colleagues and in leading and managing my staff. Oh, and it did take a few summers, but before I left for my next position, the garden had a vibrant group of gardeners and a small volunteer board that ensured its continued success long after I left. (contributed by Randall S. Hansen, PhD)

"What will they say about you?" questions

Interviewer motivation for asking: Questions that ask what others will say about you are a prelude to checking your references. Whatever you tell the interviewer had better check out with the people the interviewer plans to talk to.

Strategy for response: Be sure you know what others will say about you. This type of knowledge is a crucial part of identifying and coaching references, as described in Chapter 7, but because you will likely be asked what others would say about you, you will want to identify and coach your references well before you start interviewing. Be aware also that, through his or her network, the employer may talk to people who are not on your submitted reference list; therefore, it's incumbent upon you to have a good feel for how others perceive you. The fee-based 360°Reach Personal Brand Assessment (*www.reachbrandingclub.com/360.html*) provides an easy and inexpensive way to gather that information.

Sample questions in this subject area:

o *Describe the last constructive feedback that you received from your manager.

o What would the most recent person you've reported to say about you and your work?

o What would a colleague say about you and your work?

o What would a client say about you?

o What would a close friend say about you?

o What will your references say about you?

Sample response for this subject area:

Question: What would the most recent person to whom you've reported say about you and your work?

Response: I currently report to the senior vice president of operations, and she would tell you that I am an indispensible member of her team. She would tell you that I have that rare combination of not only being able to see the big picture—and beyond—and develop broad and sweeping long-term strategies, with the focus and skills to not only capture every detail and nuance, but also implement the operational tactics to achieve our long-term strategies. She would also tell you that I am a hard and conscientious worker, one who pushes my staff to achieve their best, while leading by example. Finally, she would say that I have risen through the ranks of my profession at a faster pace than most, but that simply reflects my intuitive knowledge and understanding—and passion—for my work. (contributed by Randall S. Hansen, PhD)

Best and worst questions

Interviewer motivation for asking: These types of questions are a bit along the lines of off-the-wall questions. Some may be job-related; others not. They are often aimed at testing how well you can think on your feet. The employer is also looking for where your passions lie and whether you will be a good fit for the targeted position.

Strategy for response: For questions directly about your career, be sure not to disparage a former employer. Be sure that your "bests" are relevant to the job you're interviewing for. The favorite book question is fairly common, so be sure you have a profession-related response to that.

Sample questions in this subject area:

- o *What was the best job you ever had?
- o *What's the worst job you've ever had?
- o What is the most difficult position you have ever held? Why? (contributed by Daniel Berger)
- o Compare and contrast the times when you did work that was above the standard with times your work was below the standard.
- o What was the best book [you've read in the last year] [you've ever read]?

Sample response for this subject area:

Question: What was the best book you've ever read?

Response: I try to read a combination of business-oriented books and books for my own personal development or simply for pleasure. I find that I can almost always learn something—something that I can apply to my personal or professional life—that makes me better, happier, more fulfilled. Because I am such an avid reader, it's also a question I ask applicants when I am the one hiring.

I just finished reading *The Brand Bubble*, a book that focuses on helping understand current trends in branding and brand loyalty and concludes with some interesting ideas on how companies can develop better branding strategies.

The one book, though, that changed my career and helped propel my thinking forward, is Seth Godin's *Purple Cow*. Some dismiss the book because it is such a quick read—but it's not so much about the length of the book as it is the book's singular message. Godin makes the point that playing it safe—being too conservative in business practices—can lead to failure. He says playing it safe is risky, and we can see many examples of that today, especially in the automotive industry. Companies need to continue to innovate, continue to monitor competitive practices and best them. One can never assume past success equates to future success. (contributed by Randall S. Hansen, PhD)

Mistake and failure questions

Interviewer motivation for asking: This line of questioning is related to the "weakness" question. The interviewer wants to see if you will take ownership for your mistakes and failures, or if you tend to blame circumstances or other people. The interviewer also wants to see what you've learned from your mistakes and failures.

Strategy for response: Pick mistakes and failures that are not devastating, and then take responsibility for them. Describe in detail what you learned and how you now not only apply that learning to your work but how it has made your work even more effective (in other words, the employer will benefit from your learning and indeed from your mistake or failure).

Sample questions in this subject area:

o *What was the last mistake that you made?

o What is the biggest mistake you've made?

o Describe a situation in which you found that your results were not up to your boss's expectations. What happened? What action did you take?

o Describe some times when you were not very satisfied or pleased with your performance. What did you do about it?

o Tell me about a time when you failed to meet a deadline. What things did you fail to do? What were the repercussions? What did you learn?

Sample response for this subject area:

Question: Describe a time when you were not very satisfied or pleased with your performance. What did you do about it?

Response: As someone who is constantly striving to improve my performance—and thus improve the results for my employer—there are many situations in which I could have performed better. But rather than dwelling on the issue, I quickly assess any flaws in my thinking or performance and make both mental and actual notes so that I learn from it and do not make the same mistake twice.

For example, last month I relied on a vendor's recommendation—one that was also supported by my team—rather than taking the time to investigate the other top options on the table. We were upgrading some of our server enhancements—nothing mission-critical—but still things that would make it easier for our customers. I was also working on a report for top management on IT infrastructure architecture upgrades—and realized shortly afterwards that I did not focus enough of my time on the decision regarding the server enhancements. What I learned from this situation is that I cannot let major projects or initiatives interfere with what can be considered lower priority decisions—that I should budget time to fully review, analyze, and perhaps question all decisions related to my division. (contributed by Randall S. Hansen, PhD)

Industry-specific questions

Interviewer motivation for asking: The interviewer wants to measure your proficiency in functions of the targeted job that are specific to this industry or field. Some questions may seem like SAT questions that test your knowledge of the industry. The sample questions in this category contributed by Dawn Boyer, director of marketing, sales, public relations, and human resources to government clients for MonsterClean in Virginia Beach, Va., are targeted at specific industries, but with a little imagination, you can conceptualize how an interviewer might adapt similar questions to your industry.

Strategy for response: Be sure you are extremely well-versed and current in the jargon in your field. Read trade publications if you feel rusty. Know what the key buzzwords are; reading job postings from employers in the field will provide a good overview. If you are changing industries, you'll have to work harder at these preparatory activities. Talk to people in your target industry to be sure you have a handle on the vocabulary. The last question in this category, "Given that you are changing industries, how long do you think it will take for you to become productive in this industry?", is a bit of a trick question. You can be *productive* right away, even if you need a little time to get up to speed on specific industry knowledge.

Sample questions in this subject area:

o Define the following industry-specific terms: _____, _____, _____, _____.

o What do the following acronyms stand for?

o What has been your experience with [industry-specific job function]?

o Our company is teetering on the brink of moving from 8(a) status, in which the federal government virtually hands over contracts to us, to where the company is moving into the full and open competition market. If we hire you into this job, what would be your short-range goals, long-range goals, and what various aspects would you have to consider to develop those goals and objectives? (contributed by Dawn Boyer)

o Thanks for considering the director of HR position with our company. We have a staff of six already, but they don't seem to be a cohesive team, and morale is weak. What would you do coming in to get the confidence of the team and to get a ROI on the salaries in that department? (contributed by Dawn Boyer)

o We have a team of business developers and marketing specialists that has been working for six years but hasn't won a full and open contract yet. What would you do first to come in and analyze what the company is doing wrong and right and get us on the right track? (contributed by Dawn Boyer)

o The company is thinking about going public; as a CPA and accountant, can you tell me what we need to do to get ready for the IPO? What do you know about Sarbanes-Oxley, and what do we need to do to become compliant before the IPO? (contributed by Dawn Boyer)

- o Given that you are changing industries, how long do you think it will take for you to become productive in this industry?

Sample response for this subject area:

Question: Given that you are changing industries, how long do you think it will take for you to become productive in this industry?

Response: I expect to be productive from Day One.

While yours is indeed a different industry from my current experience, I have three things going for me that work in my favor for transitioning quickly. First, yours is an industry I have followed for years, so while there are still significant inner workings that I am sure I have not been privy to, I am keenly aware of the major players, trends, challenges, and opportunities. Second, I plan to use the same skills that have made me successful in my current position and apply them here. Third, I have always been a quick study with a knack for cutting through the clutter to see the big picture.

I truly believe these three factors will make my learning curve much shorter than you may have imagined, and I anticipate being productive from my first day, increasing my understanding and efficiencies with each passing day. (contributed by Randall S. Hansen, PhD)

Targeted skills and competencies questions

Interviewer motivation for asking: It's a given that the interviewer will want to know how you perceive (and how you substantiate) your grasp of the skills that are relevant to the targeted position. Though these targeted skills will vary by position, and the list that follows isn't exhaustive, it encompasses skills sought by most employers of executive and senior-level candidates.

Strategy for response: Be sure you know through your research the skills the employer is most likely to ask about. Then develop S-A-R/P-A-R/C-A-R stories that show how you have successfully applied those skills.

Time-management, prioritization, organization, and planning questions

Sample questions in this subject area:

- o *How many hours a week do you find it necessary to work to get your job done?

o What's an ideal workweek for you?

o *What kinds of deadlines did/do you deal with in your last/ present job?

o *Have you ever been asked to accept additional responsibilities or work at a time when you were already maxed out?

o *I'd like for you to think about the last project or assignment that you worked on where you had tight deadlines and multiple milestones. Describe it to me.

o How do you go about planning a complex project so that it achieves objectives? What management tools do you use?

o Describe a situation that required a number of things to be done at the same time. How did you handle it? What was the result?

o Do you tend to leave your work at the office or take it home with you?

o How do you determine priorities in scheduling your time? Give examples.

o Tell me about a time you had to handle multiple responsibilities. How did you organize the work you needed to do?

o What would a particularly heavy workload look like to you?

o Describe the system you use for keeping track of multiple projects. How do you track your progress so that you can meet deadlines? How do you stay focused?

o Give me an example of when you met the personal and professional demands in your life, yet still maintained a healthy balance.

o How well organized do you consider yourself to be?

o Describe your last stressful deadlined project.

Sample response for this subject area:

Question: Tell me about a time you had to handle multiple responsibilities. How did you organize the work you needed to do?

Response: I could pull out my BlackBerry and have you look at my schedule for almost any week during the past year, and you would see that a day doesn't go by when I am not managing about three of four major projects, a few smaller undertakings, and a potential crisis or two. I thrive on tackling multiple issues, working with various colleagues and teams to deliver superior solutions. Let me talk just about last week. We have an investors' meeting coming up, and I needed to prepare a report for the CEO, so I spent considerable time meeting with the CEO and writing the report and talking points. At the same time, I was meeting with several departments to review and evaluate new product initiatives for next year. We also have a sales territory that suddenly fell off the map—managed by one of our most reliable reps. Simultaneously with these three things, of course, I handled the daily issues, such as reviewing all sales reports, responding to questions from reps, monitoring data on competitive activities, and returning emails and phone calls. At the end of the week, the CEO had the report and talking points she wanted, I finalized the set of new products that will launch next year, and—working with the entire sales team—solved the sales-territory problem. It was a great week. (contributed by Randall S. Hansen, PhD)

Problem-solving questions

Sample questions in this subject area:

- o Tell me about a major problem you recently handled. Were you successful in resolving it?
- o What was the toughest challenge you've ever faced?
- o *Describe your process for analyzing a problem that needs to be solved.
- o *What was the last problem that you had to solve on the job?
- o Describe a specific problem you solved for your employer. How did you approach the problem? What role did others play? What was the outcome?
- o *Tell me about a time when you anticipated a problem and prevented it from becoming a problem by taking preemptive action.
- o We can sometimes identify a small problem and fix it before it becomes a major problem. Give an example of how you have done this.
- o Describe an instance when you had to think on your feet to extricate yourself from a difficult situation.

- o Give me a specific example of a time when you used good judgment and logic in solving a problem.
- o Describe a time when you were faced with problems or stresses that tested your coping skills.
- o What steps do you follow to study a problem before making a decision?
- o Describe a project or situation that best demonstrates your analytical abilities.
- o What do you do when you are faced with an obstacle to an important project? Give an example.
- o Tell me about a difficult situation when it was desirable for you to keep a positive attitude. What did you do?
- o Solve this problem:_____. Or: How would you solve this problem: _____? What information and human resources would you need to solve the problem?
- o On occasion, we are confronted by dishonesty in the workplace. Tell about such an occurrence and how you handled it.

Sample response for this subject area:

Question: What was the toughest challenge you've ever faced?

Response: When I was CEO of a group of assisted-living facilities, I had a problem with the executive director. On one hand, she was brilliant and innovative, developing many initiatives that attracted new clients and raised our visibility. For example, she came up with an intergenerational program in which our residents had the opportunity to connect with young children and play grandparent roles with many of them. Knowing that family members worry about abuse to and theft from their loved ones, this executive director put webcams in residents' rooms so family members could monitor their treatment. Her innovations really put the organization on the map and helped grow the number of facilities.

However, this person was also abrasive, tactless, and completely lacking in diplomacy. She alienated employees and members of the board alike. The issue with her irritating personality came to a head when representatives from a pharmaceutical firm were touring our flagship facility because the company was considering sponsoring a new recreational program. The executive director made an extremely offensive comment about dementia patients. The worst part was that a reporter had come along on the tour, and the reporter included the remark in her coverage, prompting public outcry. I was under pressure from the board to fire this executive director. I could see their point, but I also knew how valuable her ideas were and how she had contributed to the organization's bottom line.

After asking the board to give me one more chance to rehabilitate this executive, I tackled the problem in three steps. I insisted that she write heartfelt letters of apology to those she had offended, including the employees. I then told her she must work closely with an executive coach to improve her communication skills. Finally, I promoted a mid-level manager to a new position as executive director for communications, making him the new spokesperson and public face of the company. Without really taking anything away from the executive director's position or prestige, I simply added a buffer that would keep her blunt remarks from doing further damage. The company flourished with this solution, enjoying the benefit of the executive director's brilliance while ensuring better communication.

Decision-making questions

Sample questions in this subject area:

o What criteria are you using to choose companies to interview with? (This is an employer-comprehension question as well as a decision-making question because your response should include criteria that fit the employer with whom you're interviewing.)

o Would you say that you easily deal with high-pressure situations?

o When given an important assignment, how do you approach it?

o *When was the last time you asked for help at work?

o *Have you ever made a decision at work that turned out to be the wrong one?

o What kinds of decisions have you had to make most frequently in your most recent position? How have you done so?

o *Describe your decision-making process.

o Give an example of a time in which you had to be relatively quick in coming to a decision.

o Recall a time when you were assigned what you considered to be a complex project. Specifically, what steps did you take to prepare for and finish the project? Were you happy with the outcome? What one step would you have done differently if given the chance?

o What was the most complex assignment you have had? What was your role?

o Give me an example of a time you had to make an important decision. How did you make the decision? How does it affect you today?

o Tell me about a time when you had to make a decision but didn't have all the information you needed.

o Everyone has made some poor decisions or has done something that just did not turn out right. Give an example of when this has happened to you.

o Describe a time when you had to make a difficult choice between your personal and professional life.

o Give me a specific occasion in which you conformed to a policy with which you did not agree.

o Tell of a situation in which you had to adjust quickly to changes over which you had no control. What was the impact of the change on you?

o Tell about a time when your trustworthiness was challenged. How did you react/respond?

Sample response for this subject area:

Question: Would you say that you easily deal with high-pressure situations?

Response: Yes. My sense is that my decision-making in all situations involves analyzing the situation, contemplating possible solutions—including seeking input from both my team and relevant parties, reviewing the impact of any decision on all stakeholders, moving toward a solution, seeking final input on my decision if there is time, and implementing the solution. Obviously, in high-pressure situations, both the circumstances and timing have a major impact on squeezing the decision-making process.

Let me give you an example of my decision-making in my most recent high-pressure situation. I think it's not only a good example of managing under pressure, but also my overall style of decision-making. In my current position as vice president of marketing and sales for Marvy-Nut Foods Corporation, I faced a potential major crisis when a deadly salmonella outbreak occurred with our peanut butter supplier. While the peanut butter we purchased for our Little Marvy crackers did not come from the problem plant, we had to decide whether to continue distributing the products or voluntarily recall them. We had to determine the possibility of another one of these supplier plants being infected and the risk of one or more of our customers becoming ill—or worse. And if we recalled the products, we would have a huge drop in sales revenue—and not just from the recalled products, but a ripple effect on our other items. I assembled my team on a Sunday evening, put all the information, alternatives, and potential scenarios on the table. After a fairly lively discussion—and weighing all the feedback—I brought in the president and CEO of the company, Mike Marvin, and we both agreed that we had to do the voluntary recall. (contributed by Randall S. Hansen, PhD)

Interpersonal, oral, and written communication questions

Sample questions in this subject area:

- o Are you more energized by working with data or by collaborating with other individuals?
- o How would you evaluate your ability to deal with conflict?
- o What, in your opinion, are the key ingredients in guiding and maintaining successful business relationships?
- o *Have you ever spoken up about something you knew wasn't working as well as it could? (Do you communicate ideas or keep them to yourself?)
- o *Describe your communication style.
- o *What kind of written documentation did/do you regularly produce for your last/present role?
- o *On a scale of 1-10, with 10 being highest, how would you describe your ability to write articulately in English?
- o *Describe your approach to dealing with internal and external clients.

o *Describe a time when you've had to modify your communication style to get through to someone, either at work or with a customer.

o *If we asked you to stand up and give an extemporaneous speech in front of hundreds of people, how comfortable would you be?

o What has been your experience in giving presentations? What has been your most successful experience in speech making?

o Have you ever presented to a "tough crowd?" How did you win them over?

o *Are you a people person?

o *Given your choice, would you prefer to work with others or work solo?

o Describe a situation in which you were able to use persuasion to successfully convince someone to see things your way.

o Have you ever made a judgment about someone that turned out to be a misconception? What did you do?

o Tell of a time when you had to persuade someone on a very tight timeframe.

o Describe a situation in which you delivered an unpopular communication.

o Describe a time when you had to use your written communication skills to get an important point across.

o Describe the most significant or creative presentation that you have had to complete.

o Give me an example of a time when you were able to successfully communicate with another person even when that individual may not have personally liked you (or vice versa).

o Describe a situation in which you had to arrive at a compromise or guide others to a compromise.

o How well do you interact with [people younger than you] [people of the opposite gender] [people of diverse ethnicities and cultures]?

- Tell of a time when your active listening skills really paid off for you—maybe a time when other people missed the key idea being expressed.
- Give an example of when you had to work with someone who was difficult to get along with. Why was this person difficult? How did you handle that person?
- Describe a time when you got co-workers who dislike each other to work together. How did you accomplish this? What was the outcome?
- Describe a situation where you found yourself dealing with someone who didn't like you. How did you handle it?
- Give me an example of a time you had to persuade other people to take action. Were you successful?
- Tell me about a time when you had to deal with a difficult person. How did you handle the situation?
- Give me a specific example of a time when you sold your boss on an idea or concept. How did you proceed? What was the result?
- Tell about a time when you built rapport quickly with someone under difficult conditions.
- Describe a situation where you felt you had not communicated well. How did you correct the situation?
- Describe a time when you took personal accountability for a conflict and initiated contact with the individual(s) involved to explain your actions.
- Recall a situation in which communications were poor. How did you handle it?
- Tell about the most difficult or frustrating individual that you've ever had to work with, and how you managed to work with that person.
- Tell of the most difficult experience that you have ever had to handle with a stakeholder—perhaps someone who was angry or irate. Be specific and tell what you did and what was the outcome.

o What media do you most prefer for communicating (face-to-face, phone, e-mail, and so on)?

Sample response for this subject area:

Question: Give an example of when you had to work with someone who was difficult to get along with. Why was this person difficult? How did you handle that person?

Response: When I was hired for my current position at Whirlpool, I had a division manager who was extremely negative about everything, especially when it was a new idea or concept that I was trying to initiate. I did a little research on the guy—he had a very strong reputation within the company and the people who worked for him said great things about him. It was puzzling to me. After digging a little deeper—inside those hushed conversations people have—I discovered he had been the lone internal candidate for my position. I couldn't blame him for feeling bitter and alienated; he may have even been on the job market for all I knew. But he was a great manager, and I needed to find a way to turn him around and make him part of my team. I decided this situation was best handled outside the office, so I invited him to join me for a round of golf and dinner. It took a few holes of my prodding while he was still being a bit confrontational, but as we hit the 8th or 9th hole, we started to hit some common ground. As we approached the 18th hole, he was sharing some ideas he had for improving the distribution and sales of our appliances. We continued the conversation and brainstorming over dinner. I also found a few ways to throw a few perks his way. Five years later, he is still with the company. We still butt heads at the office—but now in a good way, in which he challenges ideas to make them better rather than simply being negative. (contributed by Randall S. Hansen, PhD)

Teamwork questions

Sample questions in this subject area:

o How would you describe yourself in terms of your ability to work as a member of a team?

o Some people work best as part of a group; others prefer the role of individual contributor. How would you describe yourself?

o *Describe your current team.

o *Have you ever been on a team where there is open conflict?

o Describe a situation where others you were working with on a project disagreed with your ideas. What did you do?

o Tell of a time when you worked with a colleague who was not completing his or her share of the work.

o Describe a team experience you found disappointing. What could you have done to prevent it?

o Have you ever led a team that did not directly report to you?

Sample response for this subject area:

Question: Some people work best as part of a group—others prefer the role of individual contributor. How would you describe yourself?

Response: As I have progressed through my career, the one certainty I have discovered is that no matter the work environment, there are colleagues with amazing talents. While these folks are good individually, you put them in a team and the ideas and solutions increase dramatically. Thus, while there is always a place for individual work and achievement, I think the organization is almost always better served by team collaborations, whether in transitional work groups or permanent teams. I apply that same notion to myself, especially as a leader and manager. I know I have some expert skills and competencies, but I would be foolish to think that working as part of a team does not enhance my abilities and decision-making. So, to answer your question, I would have to say there is a place for both individual and team work, but in my experience, the results from a well-functioning team are far superior to any individual contribution—and thus I prefer taking my ideas to a team, listening to others' ideas, and then coming together to form the best solution to the problem. (contributed by Randall S. Hansen, PhD)

Integrating a portfolio into your responses

A career portfolio is a worthwhile tool to create for yourself and bring to interviews because it enables you to show tangible proof of your performance through samples of your work. Typical items that you can include in an executive career portfolio are reports; white papers; studies; brochures; projects; presentations; published papers; conference proceedings; certificates of awards and honors; testimonials from customers, clients, colleagues, and past employers; lists of conferences, seminars, and workshops you've participated in and/or attended; a listing of professional-development activities, such as professional association memberships and conferences attended; and a description of community service activities, volunteering, or pro bono work you have completed, especially as it relates to your career.

When the interviewer asks a question that calls for a response that truly demonstrates a specific skill, piece of knowledge, or accomplishment, consider presenting evidence in your portfolio. For example, the interviewer might ask you to describe the most complex project you ever oversaw. You can say, "I'd be glad to describe my most complex project. In fact, I have the project-management matrix in my portfolio. Let me walk you through that and show you photos of the key deliverables." For a question like "Do you have any experience with forecasting strategic modeling?", you could say, "Yes, I do. Let me show you the modeling spreadsheet in my portfolio."

You can also deliver a presentation in your interview (and some candidates are required to do so). See more about presentation interviews in Chapter 4.

Asking questions of the interviewer and sample questions to ask

It would be a highly unusual interview that did not end with the interviewer's offer to answer your questions. This period for your questions is a tremendous opportunity to show you've done your homework, demonstrate your intelligence and thoughtfulness, and further sell yourself. It is also, of course, your chance to pose queries that will help you decide if this role is right for you.

Be sure you have questions ready to ask. Ensure that they go beyond the superficial and the typical because your interviewer may be extremely informative and answer all the conventional questions before you even ask any. Earlier in my career, I'm sure I blew several opportunities because I often had interviewers who spent a large portion of the interview describing the specifics of the job. When they asked me if I had any questions, I usually told them they had answered them all. Ask questions that help you understand the job better, and once the interviewer responds, apply your new understanding to a story that describes a selling point germane to your response.

Do not ask questions that could easily be answered through your research. At this point, also do not ask questions about salary, benefits, and perks. Here is a list of insightful questions to provide a starting place for you to develop your own queries:

o   What is the top priority of the person who accepts this job?

o   Can you describe a typical day for someone in this position? What are the day-to-day expectations and responsibilities of this job?

o   How will my leadership responsibilities and performance be measured? And by whom? How often?

o   Can you discuss your take on the company's corporate culture?

o   How would you describe the company's values?

o   Can you describe the company's management style?

o   How would you characterize the management philosophy of this organization? Of your department?

o   What is the organization's policy on transfers to other divisions or other offices?

o   Are lateral or rotational job moves available?

o   Does the organization support ongoing training and education for employees to stay current in their fields?

o   What do you think is the greatest opportunity facing the organization in the near future? The biggest threat?

o   Why did you come to work here? What keeps you here?

o   How is this department perceived within the organization?

o   Is there a formal process for advancement within the organization?

o   What are the traits and skills of people who are the most successful within the organization?

Hiring decision-makers shared favorite questions that they had asked in interviews or heard candidates ask. Outsourced HR professional Nichole Woody of Professional Placement Services in Solon, Ohio, suggests asking, "What activities does this company involve itself in within the local community?" (for example, participation in a food bank, Relay for Life, sponsorship of youth sports groups, adopt a park/highway). Woody points out that such a question "will tell you as a candidate a lot about the organization's values and level of social responsibility." As Woody notes, asking this question shows the interviewer you are not limited to working within the requirements of your role, "but will extend their [community-service] efforts wherever possible."

Daniel Dildine, a network services technician at the Industrial Commission of Ohio in Columbus, says his favorite question to ask a future employer is "Do you like working here?" Dildine says he doubts that he would want to take a job "where the interviewer was not immediately positive with the answer."

"If I were to start the position tomorrow, what could I do to immediately make your job easier?" is the favorite question of Sara Allred, sales and recruiting manager for DirectLink, Las Vegas, Nev. Alejandro Prieto, account manager at MA Labs, wants to know about how the organization motivates its people and asks, "If I get the job, how do you get the best out of me? What do you do to get the best out of your employees?"

Difna Blamey, head of human resources at Screwfix Ltd., Bath, United Kingdom, offers a list of questions taken from her experience as both an interviewer and interviewee.

If you are interviewed by the hiring manager:

o What about this organization keeps you awake at night?

o What is your team famous for? What do you want them to be famous for?

o How do you get your team working well together?

o If you were the CEO of this organization, what two or three things would you change?

o How do people know if they're achieving outstanding performance? That is, what would I need to achieve?

o What mechanisms/processes are in place that enable the team to receive feedback from customers? What has the most recent feedback been?

o What is the toughest decision this business had to make in the past six months and what was the output?

If you are interviewed by human resources or others who are not the hiring decision-maker, Blamey recommends these questions:

- What are the two or three things that I won't like about working here?
- How does this business retain good people?
- How does good performance get recognized here?
- What was the one area that surprised you most about this business when you joined?
- How have you been developed in your role to achieve higher performance?
- How does this business celebrate its successes?
- What are your customers saying about this business? How is this information captured and distributed?

Asking Questions That Inspire the Hire

Dawn Boyer has turned asking questions of the interviewer into an art form. "I have been interviewed in the past where I knew that the interviewer wanted to hire me on the spot because of the questions I posed during the interview," Boyer says. Not only do her questions impress hiring decision-makers enough to make her job offers, but the responses she gleans help her decide if the employer is a good fit for her. "The experience I've had in past employment and companies has opened my eyes to the type of organizations for which I wish to work," Boyer says, "and the answers to these questions usually provide the information that would assist in making a decision to work for a company with good answers."

Here are the questions Boyer plans to ask her next set of prospective employers in the human resources field:

- Does your organization have a code of ethics? And is the organization involved in corporate volunteerism and the community?
- Is the organizational practice compliant with Sarbanes-Oxley, even if it does not have to be legally?

o Does the decision-making authority in the company hinder or help the company and its employees grow in response to new technology and/or organizational changes?

o What is the organization's corporate strategy now, and in the future?

o What HR technology does the company use for its recruiting, HRIS (Human Resource Information System), e-learning, employment documentation and record retention, and application service providers (online benefit enrollment, for example)?

o Which classification/compensation system is in place now? When was the last update? What is the frequency of aging, salary updates with cost-of-living allowance?

o Compliance: Does the organization conduct internal and/or external audits regularly?

o What are the most recent HR projects that are championed by upper C-level managers?

o Is the organization/hiring manager seeking a change agent, a stability facilitator, or an organizational developer for this position?

o Is the organization/hiring manager seeking someone who will focus on interpersonal, technological, or structural relationships within the organization and the position being filled?

o Is Total Quality Management/ISO in place? When was the most recent certification, if in place? What are future projected efforts in the direction of certification?

o What trade organizations does management actively engage in?

Your interview as a sales call: Content for overcoming objections and closing the sale

The best executive candidates understand the power of marketing in the job search. Comparing your job interview to a sales call is vital to achieving success in obtaining the job offers you seek. But the burden is not all on the candidate because the employer also sees the job interview as a sales call—and just as much as you are selling yourself as the product that you want the employer to purchase, the hiring manager is also selling the employer's value to you.

Anyone who knows even just a little about sales knows that the key to success is in overcoming objections and then closing the sale. You can do the same in the job interview—and using this technique will take you one step closer to the job offer.

Overcoming objections

A proven sales theory is that if you can overcome all your prospect's objections, the prospect will have no choice but to agree to your offer. The logic holds that if you overcome all the objections of the hiring manager, you'll be more likely to move on to the next step in the process.

You can overcome objectives in a number of ways, but the keys are to acknowledge the interviewer's objection, understand the true root of the objection, and respond with enough information to defuse the objection. It's best to anticipate these potential objections before the interview so that you can practice your responses.

In attempting to overcome these objections remember not to dwell on the objection, but instead, once you are sure you understand it, turn it around to overcome it. If the interviewer has uncovered an Achilles' heel, find a way to turn it into a strength. For example, if you were fired from your last job, find a way to showcase how the experience has given you new insight into making sure your boss knows the contributions you are making.

What do you do if the interviewer raises no objections? It might not mean that the employer has none, so it's best to probe to uncover any—again, because it's much better to get them out in the open and address them than to let them sit, clouding your future. As the interview winds down, if the interviewer has raised no objections or concerns, consider asking a question such as, "Do you see any concerns that stand in the way of my succeeding in this position?"

Common objections from employers

Here's a collection of some of the more common objections raised in job interviews.

"I'm concerned you are overqualified for this position." This comment is the most loaded of objections because it can mean one of several things—and it is your job to discover which one it is. The good news is that if you are in the interview, your qualifications have made you an attractive candidate. This comment often conceals a concern about your age, attitude, or motivation. Obviously the interviewer cannot ask your age, but someone with significant experience is often mature, and the employer may have some concerns about fit, especially if the rest of the department is younger. Older workers also sometimes put out a vibe that because of their vast experience they know it all—and are seen as having an attitude problem. Finally, if you have years in the same type of position, some interviewers will question your drive and motivation to move ahead (incorrectly assuming that everyone wants to do so).

"I'm just not sure you have the experience for this position." On the other side of the spectrum is a candidate who shows potential—and thus gets the interview—but with whom the employer has some lingering doubts, especially if you are changing fields. Your goal is to show exactly how—regardless of the time spent or where it was spent—that you have the skills to get the job done. An effective tool for this objection is a career portfolio, in which you not only can tell the story of how you are qualified—but show it through examples in your portfolio.

"I'm not sure you would fit into the team." So many jobs require workers to participate in one or more teams that it seems inconceivable that a candidate would not have experience working in teams, but if for some reason you lack experience in teamwork or don't come off as a team player, you must demonstrate that you understand the importance of teams in the workplace and how you can be a team player. Demonstrating your knowledge of the organizational culture will also be a plus in this situation.

"I'm concerned about the number of jobs you've held in such a short period." If you have had an unusual number of jobs in the last few years, some interviewers will raise the job-hopper question, so you need to be able to explain the logic of your job history. It's important to note that even though employers are not as loyal to their employees as in the past, they still expect employee loyalty.

"We really like you but are just not sure where you fit." The good news about this objection is that you have won half the battle because the employer likes you and wants to hire you but is simply unsure of how to best utilize your skills. The key to your response has to be having the confidence in yourself and the knowledge about the employer to explain clearly why you are a fit for the position you are interviewing for.

Another common objection, **"We're concerned because you were fired from your last job."** is covered in Chapter 6.

Another Perspective on Objections: The Sense-Able Stumper Solution Strategy

Judy Rosemarin notes that when candidates hear interviewers make a statement "that often is misunderstood as an objection," they often become dejected or defensive. For example, candidates may interpret the "overqualified" comment as a polite dismissal at best or a flat-out rejection at worst. Rosemarin says the effect on an executive hearing this statement is much like a deer in the headlights: stunned and stymied, by this "stumper." Here is Rosemarin's view on how to handle the stumper:

"All too often, executives will come back and respond to a stumper by saying, 'Yes, but ...' and take a defensive stance without even knowing what the underlying concern is. They assume the worst.

"Executives need to understand that the words are only the surface verbalization. The real energy is underneath, rolled into thoughts, feelings, worries, and concerns, which, for myriad reasons (not the least of which is they fear making the wrong decision), no interviewer will come out and tell you directly. So, they camouflage their concerns with a stumper.

"Other forms of stumpers include, 'You have been in the same company for 12 years' or 'You don't have experience in this industry.'

"Your first job is to not react defensively but try to guess—and you do not have to be correct—what the interviewer's underlying concerns *might* be when you hear, 'You may be overqualified.'

"'*Might*' is the driver in your thinking. What *might* the interviewer be concerned about underneath the surface stumper? Making a quick guess-list of three things an interviewer might be worried about might include concern that (a) you might not stay, (b) you might be too costly (3) you might be set in your ways.

"Respond to that stumper with a question that will tease out the unexpressed concern so you can keep a conversation going and connect you to those unexpressed concerns. Here is the linguistic structure that not only works every time, but doesn't have to represent the correct guess about the interviewer's underlying concern: 'If you are concerned [that I might not stay] [that I might be too costly] [that I might be set in my ways], I would like to tell you that I have always been a troubleshooter and dedicated to my firms, looking to successfully identify places where continuous improvement can be made in every position I have ever had.'

"Here's the magic of what happens next. If you are correct in your guess that the concern focused on staying at the company, then you have informed the nervous interviewer that you are indeed a viable candidate for the job. You have given the interviewer more than he or she may have expected. Good. If, however, your speculation was off, guess what? When the interviewer hears you say, 'If you are concerned about....' he or she now has to let you know what the real concern was.

"If the real concern was something different from your guess, your statement forces the interviewer to reveal the actual concern. It might sound like, 'No, I am not concerned about that, but we are not sure that we have the budget for what you may be seeking.'

"There! You helped him or her reveal it! Now you can talk about his or her concern. You have unearthed it in a graceful and elegant way, with everyone saving face, and you have successfully kept from becoming that deer frozen in headlights."

Closing the sale

Once you have made your salient points about how you are the perfect candidate for the position and overcome objections from the interviewer, your final step is closing the sale. How aggressive you are in this step is sometimes the difference between an offer and nothing, but it is up to you to decide how strongly to close the interview. At a minimum, employ what marketers might call the trial close. Ask about the next step in the process, how many other candidates the hiring manager expects to interview, and an estimate of the timetable for completing the process. If you truly feel the interview was strong, that you are a great fit for the position, and that you have overcome all the interviewer's objections, consider asking for the job. That doesn't mean you should ask in a begging or groveling way, but that you should summarize what you believe the employer seeks in the person hired, express confidence that you meet those qualifications, and tell the interviewer that you would love to come on board.

Finally, always remember that the interview really is a conversation between two parties who are both trying to showcase their best points. Your goal is to leave the interview knowing you did your best to sell your unique mix of skills and accomplishments while overcoming any objections raised.

6

Executive-Interview Conundrums

Job interviewing can be an unnerving experience, but if you know how to handle some of the stickiest situations you might encounter, you can be that much more confident. In this chapter, career and interview coaches, as well as hiring decision-makers, provide advice about some of these situations.

Handling pre-employment screenings and assessments

Executive-level employers are increasingly using pre-screening and assessment techniques early in the interviewing process—typically after one or more initial phone screenings and before the first face-to-face interview or between the first and second interview. Sometimes they are used only when the field is narrowed down to just a few candidates. Ira Wolfe, author and president of Success Performance Solutions, cites surveys that indicate more than 80 percent of Fortune 500s use assessments for executive positions and says that small businesses also use them. "Utilization, however, is growing," Wolfe says.

Executive recruiter Lorne Epstein, who conducts these screening procedures on behalf of his client employers, says the purpose of the pre-screens and assessments is to "assure the company is hiring a reliable and qualified manager/executive." Epstein adds that because hiring decision-makers are "trusting the future of the company in [candidates'] hands with little or no direct experience of their professional ability," testing prospective hires is good business. John M. Beane, president of Staff Development Services in Leland, N.C., notes that an appropriate assessment can provide information about how well a candidate "can handle the tasks associated with the position and how will he or she handle the people."

"Many companies are looking beyond just past credentials and past experience to using pre-hire assessments," says Jan Margolis, founder and managing director of Metuchen, New Jersey-based Applied Research Corporation," which are more accurate predictors of future success or derailment in a new job and work culture."

Experts also point to the objectivity of these methods and the notion that they prevent hiring decision-makers from being influenced by what Epstein calls "the candidate's charisma or ability to persuade." The use of pre-employment screenings and assessments has increased, Beane notes, because "as people have become better educated, they have also become increasingly manipulative of their personal information." Beane discounts the value of resumes because of "people taking credit for things they did not do or claim[ing] educational backgrounds that may not exist."

"An objective third-party assessment is a useful aid in selection decisions as it objectively identifies and describes the executive's job-relevant characteristics, such as their personal style, ways of delegating, making decisions and problem-solving," Margolis says. "It does not evaluate professional or technical qualifications, but rather, focuses on the executive's capacity to lead and manage others effectively."

Assessments may measure such areas as skills, behaviors, motivation, and attitudes, says Norm Bobay, president of hireMAX, Fort Worth, Tex.

Another area sometimes assessed is honesty and integrity. Am‹
pre-screens and assessments that employers may require are:

- o *Predictive Index*, which Epstein describes as "an onl...‹
  survey that tells me what type of person the candidate is and
  how he or she works with others as well as what's going in his
  of her life now."

- o *Kolbe A Index*, which measures a person's instinctive method
  of operation, and identifies the ways he or she will be most
  productive.

- o *Occupational Personality Questionnaire*, a work styles
  assessment for managerial and professional staff that assesses
  31 behavioral dimensions.

- o *Hogan Development Survey*, identifies personality-based
  performance risks and derailers of interpersonal behavior that
  affect an individual's leadership style and actions. [*http://
  www.hoganassessments.com/assessments-hogan-
  development-survey*]

- o *Myers-Briggs Type Indicator*, is a well-known personality
  assessment, the use of which in hiring is controversial at best.
  The Myers-Briggs "is not intended for hiring or job-candidate
  selection, and...its use as a hiring tool is unethical," says an
  article by Douglas P. Shuit on the Workforce Management
  Website (*www.workforce.com/section/06/feature/23/57/09/
  index.html*), citing Michael Segovia, director of business
  development at CPP Inc., publishers of the Myers-Briggs.

- o *Simmons Personal Survey*, which measures job-related
  emotional and behavioral tendencies, such as energy, stress,
  optimism, self-esteem, commitment to work, attention to
  detail, desire for change, physical courage, self-direction,
  assertiveness, tolerance, consideration for others, and
  sociability. [*http://www.eqhelp.com/Company2a.htm*]

- o *The Executive Achiever*, which looks at intelligence,
  knowledge of leadership skills, and a variety of leadership
  personality traits. [*http://www.selectionresources.com/
  executive_achiever/index.cfm*]

o *Profiles*, which gauges cognitive, behavioral, and connative (occupational interests) attributes. [*http://www.profilesinternational.com/hww_about.aspx*]

o *Caliper Profile*, which measures more than 25 personality traits that relate to job performance. [*http://www.caliperonline.com/assessments-consulting.asp*]

o *SmartAssessment*, which Thor Mann, principal with ghSMART, the management-assessment firm behind SmartAssessment, says comprises "a straightforward 4.5-hour biographical interview that captures themes related to fit for a role from childhood through all stages of education and each and every job the candidate has had." Candidates are rated according to their probability of success in the role, Mann says. [*www.ghsmart.com*]

o *Five-factor personality assessments*, a variety of assessments that measure the "Big Five" personality traits: openness, conscientiousness, extraversion, agreeableness, and neuroticism (sometimes known as emotional stability). [*http://www.personalityresearch.org/bigfive.html*]

o *DiSC*, which profiles four primary behavioral styles (dominance, influence, steadiness, and conscientiousness) each with a distinct and predictable pattern of observable behavior. [*http://www.onlinediscprofile.com/?gclid=CIKg8eWOxJoCFRk_awodWFIgsA*]

o *Business Values and Motivators*, based on the premise that if the job or culture is valued, employees will be motivated; this assessment tells what employees value. [*http://www.super-solutions.com/business-values-and-motivators.asp*]

o *Key Management Dynamics Assessment* from Objective Management Group, designed specifically for the executive team and candidates for executive leadership positions. It measures nine styles and 16 qualities. [*http://www.objectivemanagement.com*]

o *Questionnaires and essay-style applications*. Epstein uses one with five to 10 questions that "asks the candidate to describe in detail what they did, how they did it, and what challenges they overcame." The questionnaire enables recruiters and employers "to dig deeper in the interview," Epstein says. Social networking strategist David Nour recommends asking candidates to profile a leader or executive after which they wish to model themselves. [*http:// www.recruitingtrends.com/online/thoughtleadership/ 1400-1.html*]

o   Speaker and hiring expert Karl Ahlrichs notes that essay-style applications "instantly screen out people who don't want to invest time" in the employer's hiring process and "help identify people who are likely to fit into the organization."

In addition to these types of assessments, Wolfe notes that general reasoning or cognitive tests to evaluate how quickly candidates can process new information and evaluate complex scenarios are gaining popularity.

Candidates should be aware of what they're getting into before undergoing pre-screens and assessments. Susan Guarneri, whose tagline is "Career Assessment Goddess," suggests that candidates consider requesting information on the purpose of the assessment as well as its validity and reliability. Calling such a request a "delicate issue to bring up," Guarneri recommends "reading the situation and using good judgment." Citing assessments like the Myers-Briggs that are not intended for candidate selection in the hiring process, Guarneri states that "just because the assessment is routinely used by a company and has not been challenged legally does not necessarily make it reliable and valid for hiring purposes." At the very least, Guarneri says, "the candidate needs to inquire about privacy practices for retention of the assessment results, as well as the test-taking situation." While Epstein assures candidates that assessments are safe and private, with information shared with no one, Guarneri advises: "You have the right to understand the criteria for pre-selection, the rationale for the use of the assessment, and the measures that will be taken to safeguard your privacy."

The degree to which you can prepare for pre-screens and assessment varies with the method used. In fact, many assessments are designed so that the user cannot prepare for them. You can, however, ensure that you are well-rested, Guarneri advises, and that you take the assessment in quiet, private surroundings. If the employer requires multiple assessments, she suggests that the candidate avoid assessment burn-out by taking time in between to stretch, get something to drink, and mentally unwind before proceeding to the next assessment. Try to skim the assessment so you have an idea of how much time to devote to each question or section. During the assessment, apply the techniques you normally summon to subdue stress and keep yourself relaxed.

For the questionnaire and essay-style methods, Epstein advises candidates to keep a journal of their successes and past work accomplishments "so they can give a detailed and accurate account of what they did and with whom they did it." Epstein notes that his firm checks this information with their references later on.

While undergoing the assessment or pre-screen, "candidates should give as much detail as possible and always be truthful," Epstein advises.

Guarneri agrees: "Do not try to 'game' the test by responding with answers you believe will make you look like a better candidate. Why contort yourself through your answers into something you are not? You will be doing a disservice to yourself, as well as the prospective employer. Instead, by responding honestly and with your first gut-level reaction, you will be revealing the 'real you' that either will be a good fit with the job and organization—or not. Answer the questions according to how you actually are and not how you would like to be." Wolfe adds, "Creating a false image of who you are may get you hired, but success and satisfaction in the job will be hit-or-miss."

Wolfe assures candidates that "there are no right or wrong responses on personality, behavior, values, and attitude assessments. He notes that when these assessments are properly used, "candidates are merely matched against benchmarks that demonstrate patterns of other executives who have been successful. By comparing individual results to a baseline, candidates can be evaluated for job, team, and culture fit. Wolfe also points out that "assessments benefit the candidate as much as the company. Being hired for a job that will only result in missed expectations benefits neither the candidate nor the organization."

"If the information gleaned from an assessment is confirmed in the interview and the candidate doesn't appear to be a good fit for the job, team, and/or culture, then the candidate might be excluded," Wolfe says. Be aware, though, that as Dave Kurlan points out, "Legally, an assessment cannot be the sole reason for ending a candidate's consideration." Kurlan, who is the founder and CEO of Objective Management Group, Inc., in Westboro, Mass., points out, "background, references, track record, industry fit, the phone conversation, intelligence, skills, the interview, and chemistry should all play a part, as well." Similarly, Wolfe says the assessment makes up "only a third of the total rating on the candidate. The remaining two-thirds comes from the interview and the resume/background checks."

Darleen DeRosa, PhD, managing partner at Onpoint Consulting in Connecticut, says some common reasons that organizations choose not to proceed with a candidate include "concern over leadership ability (person may be very strong functionally or technically, but lacks effective leadership skills); concern about cultural fit or team fit (person may not be collaborative when culture emphasizes this, or the person might not work well on a senior team due to style), or the person lacks self-awareness and may not be able to change his/her behaviors." Wolfe reassures candidates that "many times, exclusion isn't because the candidate isn't highly qualified, but the organization may not be ready for a candidate with advanced talents and skills. Candidates aren't always excluded because they don't make the grade, but because the organization is not advanced enough for them."

If you find that you are getting screened out of the interview process after undergoing a pre-screen or assessment, consider working with an executive or career coach. "Many people feel they have the character traits to be an executive, but few actually have them," observes Beane. "If only one person can be chosen, then the person having the best interview, background references, and came out best on the assessment would get the job," he says.

An excellent resource on handling pre-employment screenings and assessments is the chapter on that subject in *Interview Magic* by Susan Britton Whitcomb (JIST Publishing, 2005).

Building rapport in the interview

Very little is more important in an interview than establishing rapport with the interviewer. Why? Because employers want to hire people who are likeable, with whom they have chemistry, and who will fit in with the team. I have seen time and again that if chemistry and rapport are lacking in the interview, the candidate probably won't move to the next step in the process. Rapport is a tricky proposition because if it's not instantly present, it's not easy to establish. So how do you create chemistry and build rapport?

You'll boost your ability to build rapport if you arrive early enough for the interview that you can relax, visit the restroom, make sure you look professional, collect your thoughts about your top selling points, and observe the workplace to give yourself extra conversation fodder with the interviewer. Conversely, if you arrive at the last minute and are rushed and stressed, the interviewer will likely pick up a negative vibe, and you won't have any opportunity to absorb your surroundings. Your nonverbal behaviors—your smile, handshake, and the way you carry yourself (as discussed in Chapter 3)—will also contribute to your chemistry with the interviewer.

Expressing genuine interest in the interviewer, the job, and the organization will aid your likeability. The research described in Chapter 2 will also pay off. "Before the interview, conduct research on the interviewer so that you will have some background information and can bring up topics of mutual interest," advises executive career coach Beverly Harvey of HarveyCareers.com. "Check with your network and your network's network to see if anyone knows the interviewer and can give you some background information. Do a search on LinkedIn for people who currently work at the company, and check all their contacts to see who you might have in common. Do a Google search and see if you can find publications, articles, press releases, or a blog written by the interviewer," Harvey suggests. Executive career coach Cheryl Palmer, whose company is Call to Career, agrees that you should "identify points of interest that you have in common with the interviewer and make sure that you weave in the information that you researched early in the interview to build rapport with the interviewer. For example, if the interviewer says to you, 'Tell me about yourself,' you could respond by saying, 'Well, I have an MBA from Stanford, and I was interested to see that you graduated from Stanford also.' By showing that you have done your homework on the interviewer, you can establish that point of connection because the two of you have something in common." "Having done your research prior to the interview, you can compliment the interviewer based on information you've uncovered through your research," Harvey says. "If he or she presented at a conference, won an award, led a fundraising drive, or caught the largest fish on a charter trip, mention that you saw an article about the accomplishment. If you identified any common interests such as belonging to the same associations, you can mention your mutual interests."

Career transition consultant and author Billie Sucher, suggests using the "3 T's" of interviewing to build rapport:

1. Thank you. By starting your conversation with these two simple words "thank you," you may be one of only a handful of candidates who take the time to mind your manners. Just like a good speech, you will want to remember to express your thanks and appreciation to the people who are listening to you. In the case of executive interviews, your audience is the selection team.

2. Time. Clarify with the selection team leader your understanding of how much time you have together. Just because the recruiter said you would have two hours doesn't make it so. Do not assume anything. Clarify the timetable at the beginning of your conversation; a 90-minute conversation will proceed much differently from an abbreviated 20-minute meet-and-greet.

3. Talent. By asking one simple question, you can "sell to need" throughout the interview. The candidate asks: "Can you share with me the qualifications you desire for your new [name of position]?" Once you have heard the selection team's input, you can then "sell to need" throughout the balance of your meeting.

"Stay focused on the interviewer's needs," advises Judy Rosemarin, president of Sense-Able Strategies, Inc., New York City. "Listen to their key words and use them when you respond to their questions." Some experts go even further and suggest a "mirroring technique," in which the interviewee adapts his or her body language and speech patterns to the interviewer's so the decision-maker perceives the candidate as similar to himself or herself. Other career gurus decry this technique as coming off in a phony way. If you have a sales background, you have likely been taught this technique. If you do it well and have found it effective, you can likely apply it to interviewing effectively.

Palmer recommends observing the interviewer's office. "There may be other points of interest that you can bring up, such as sports awards and fraternal organizations." Rosmarin agrees, saying, "Notice the clues and cues of who they are, as most people mark their space with what is important to them. If you see an office that is pristine, lacking plants, books, photos, you can be pretty sure that executive, bottom-line answers will suit that person more than one with more detail."

Handling a poor interviewer

Not every professional who conducts executive interviews with candidates knows how to conduct an interview effectively. In fact, some are downright lousy at it. Even in a miserable interview situation, Rosemarin advises, "keep your focus on making the interviewer feel comfortable with you. Avoid movies in your head about how lousy the interviewer is and how he or she is not letting you do your rehearsed pitch. Stay in the moment with her or him and address his or her needs, not yours."

A bad interviewer might be unfocused, disinterested, or unprepared. He or she might dominate the interview by doing all the talking or might ask inappropriate and illegal questions (See Chapter 5).

The unfocused, unprepared interviewer probably hasn't read your resume and maybe can't even find a copy. This hapless soul doesn't even know what to ask you. Be sure to offer this disorganized interviewer a copy of your resume while asking, "May I take you through some highlights of my career?"

Some interviewers love listening to themselves talk. Once in an interview, the woman interviewing me barely asked any questions or let me get a word in. Amazingly, she offered me the job, and I heard from an insider that she had really liked me. Of course she liked me! Her experience of the interview consisted of listening to herself talk and basking in her own wonderfulness. I didn't accept the position because the interview had left me with a very "off" feeling that I would not enjoy working with this self-absorbed woman. While the bigmouth interviewer is holding forth, make as many mental notes as you can (or jot them down if you've brought a small notepad). Don't show your exasperation; instead be an attentive listener and hang on the interviewer's every word. Try to get a word in edgewise by leaning forward and opening your mouth slightly, advises Anne Kadet on Smartmoney.com. [*http:// www.smartmoney.com/spending/deals/working-interview-blues-9888/*] If that doesn't work, even a nonstop talker will likely eventually ask if you have any questions. At that point, you can ask questions or describe your fit with the company and the position based on the mental or written notes you've been making.

"Given that so many interviewers are not particularly good at asking questions or drilling down for the gold, I work with all of my coaching clients to create a checklist of points they need to communicate *no matter what,*" says professional development speaker and author Rob Sullivan. "This way, before answering any particular question, the candidate can mentally review the checklist for a great story or example that hasn't yet been discussed."

Sullivan suggests that if the interviewer has spent inordinate time asking "ridiculous" questions like "What are your weaknesses?" and "Where do you see yourself in five years?", "the candidate can take charge." When about 15 minutes remain in the interview, Sullivan recommends saying: "I noticed we are running out of time. There are a few points I'd like to share as they relate to why I am a great fit for this position. With your permission, I'd like to share those with you now."

In Sullivan's experience, "the interviewer is likely to breathe a gigantic sigh of relief because what you have essentially said is, 'I am about to make your job really easy. I'm going to tell you what I think is most important without your having to ask. You can decide if it's compelling enough.'" The strategy is also effective, Sullivan says, "because it demonstrates confidence and leadership on the candidate's part."

Similarly, career consultant Jane Finkle of Career Visions, Philadelphia, Pa., says that "candidates may be caught off guard when the individual conducting the interview is not prepared for the give-and-take of the interview process. This deficient preparation can be an advantage to the interviewee since it provides a unique opportunity to put oneself in a position of control over the interview, and, simultaneously give relief and support to an employer who may be uncomfortable in the interviewer role." Finkle's advice when an interviewer talks incessantly or follows answers with long silences is to consider intervening to refocus the interviewer's attention on you. "To seize back the interview and take center stage by refocusing the interview on your talents, skills and successes, Finkle suggests a simple query: "May I ask you a question?" followed by, for example: "May I tell you more about my latest success launching a new product?" Still, Finkle cautions that you "may need to diplomatically interrupt the interviewer with an example from personal experience that relates to one of the topics expressed in the interviewer's monologue. If you are really interested in the position, speak up with grace and poise, and don't allow the interviewer to make you invisible."

"Come prepared with your talking points, and make sure that you get those talking points in, regardless of the skill of the interviewer," Harvey advises. " If you know what you want to say before you get to the interview, you can guide the discussion to the points that you want to make. You should have already reviewed the vacancy announcement for the job and made a match in your own mind between the job's requirements and your qualifications. Make sure that you make that connection for the interviewer to show that you are well qualified for the position."

Further, "if the interviewer is rambling on about sports or the news, gently guide the conversation back to the interview by asking questions that relate to the accomplishments on which you want to expound," Harvey advises. She suggests then asking the interviewer if the employer would benefit from a result like the one the accomplishment represents.

Another problematic interviewer seems busy, preoccupied, distracted and continues to glance at e-mail and allow interruptions from phone calls and visitors during the interview. In her book *Job Search Debugged*, author and coach Rita Ashley suggests asking the harried interviewer if he or she would like to reschedule, thus politely pointing out the inappropriateness of his or her behavior.

Explaining employment gaps

Most candidates worry—with good reason—about periods of unemployment in their job histories. If you've made it to the interview stage despite obvious gaps in your resume, you will be expected to explain them in the interview. "Always fill in the gaps," Palmer advises. Calling gaps "a major red flag for employers," Palmer cautions candidates not to leave any periods between employment unexplained. "If you weren't working for pay during a certain period of time, talk about what you did during that timeframe. Make sure that employers know that you were doing something productive during the period of unemployment."

Productive activities when unemployed might include enhancing your education, undertaking consulting work, taking on contract projects, serving as a corporate or nonprofit board member, or even volunteering. When you consult during gaps in employment, Harvey explains, you can in the interview "explain the type of consulting, types of clients and their results." Even travel and hobbies can be framed as worthwhile activities. Harvey relates two client case studies to illustrate ways of explaining employment gaps:

Case 1: Jim decided to take off a year following his termination (because of an acquisition) from a fast-paced, high-stress company. He traveled, pursued his hobby, and did some volunteer work. He explained his gap by highlighting the countries he visited and the type of photography he did while traveling. Some of his photography work had been published, and he mentioned where and when. He explained his volunteer work, including Hurricane Katrina relief efforts for New Orleans families. He then mentioned the industry-related conferences that he had continued to attend and guided the interview back to his professional accomplishments.

Case 2: Walt took early retirement and five years later decided he wanted to return to corporate. Walt had done volunteer work for four organizations at various times during his retirement. He highlighted the results he drove for two of the organizations and detailed the skills he used and honed in the other two.

Gaps also may not be as great a concern as they once were. "In today's world — many executives' work patterns look at bit spotty," observes Patty DeDominic, managing partner with DeDominic & Associates, a business-consulting firm. "This was considered a fluke when I started my employment services firm in 1979, but more commonly today, good people may have had a career that makes them look more like *actors*—leading roles and supporting roles," DeDominic says.

Explaining reasons for leaving a current job

If you interview while employed, it is virtually inevitable that you will be asked why you want to leave your current job. If you are not employed, you'll likely be asked why you left your last job. While you can say you discovered your fit with the organization was not right or you had differing views from key members of the leadership team, remember never to disparage a current or past employer. Always speak positively about past and present employers even if your experience has not been positive with them. Another good response in this situation is to say that you determined you had grown as much as you could in that job and you are ready for new challenges.

"Be honest," Harvey advises. She explains how to finesse several possible explanations:

- If you are unhappy with your compensation, explain that you are feeling undervalued and are pursuing greater challenges.

- If you are unhappy because you haven't been promoted, explain that you are underutilized and that you are looking for a position that will capitalize on your talents.

- If you were promoted to a new position and are not getting along with your boss, explain that you and your boss have irreconcilable differences regarding how the company or business unit should be run.

- If your company was acquired and underwent a management change, explain that a new management team was brought in, and you're no longer in alignment with the team's vision, mission, or philosophies.

- Barb Poole, president of Hire Imaging, suggests that when leaving or planning to leave an organization, executives prepare an exit narrative as part of their suite of strategic communication documents. "It will serve as your press-release template to tell the world about your transition," Poole explains. "It should be brief, non-defensive, and positive. It can let others know that your exit was beyond your control or was a positive, forward movement. Weave that exit narrative into a succinct message of what you can do for the potential employer in an interview situation." Poole offers the following as an exit narrative for the candidate who voluntarily leaves a job:

  After a fast-track path that most recently involved heading BDC through an aggressive turnaround, revitalization and return to profitability, I worked myself out of a challenge! I'm now ready to do what I do for [potential employer]. I've done my homework and have a sense that my talents are the perfect fit in leading your resurgence back to leading your niche market.

  "Complementary to the exit narrative is the positioning narrative," Poole says. "This statement succinctly summarizes and sells you, the executive, your successes, your strengths, your goals—and how they align with the potential employer's needs. You should be able to crisply recite it in under a minute."

Explaining a termination or other job loss

Unless the employer has inside information about you—or you are currently unemployed while job-hunting—the interviewer may not know you've been terminated. However, if you have been downsized or fired from your last job, you should at least anticipate being asked about the circumstances.

It's always uncomfortable to be asked your reasons for leaving a job from which you were terminated. It's common to be defensive about the subject since no one likes being fired—even if you were let go simply because your job was eliminated—so put that defensiveness behind you when responding to questions on this topic. Don't lie about it, but don't dwell on it either. You could explain that you and the company were not a good fit; hence your performance suffered. Or that you and your boss had differing viewpoints. Emphasize what you learned from the experience that will prevent you from repeating it and ensure that you will perform well in the future.

When explaining the reason for a termination, "be brief," Harvey advises. "Keep your response upbeat, and present it as a mutually beneficial experience. In other words, don't blame your boss, the CEO, or others in the company. If you loved the job, accentuate what a wonderful opportunity it was and why, talk about your accomplishments, and simply explain that your resignation or termination was an unfortunate turn of events," she says. "Explain that if this new company hires you," Rosemarin suggests, "it will benefit from what you can do since the new management at the old company valued other things."

Poole proposes the following as a model for an exit narrative for an involuntary termination:

ABC recently changed corporate direction and reorganized. A number of senior-executive roles were eliminated, including mine. With my 22-year record of leading cost containment and improving profits for Fortune electronics companies, I'm now exploring opportunities where that background is valued and needed.

"If you can't talk about your termination without shame, anger, or hostility," Harvey advises, "you may want to consider working with a grief counselor or someone who can help you process the emotions."

Elaborating in the face of probing questions (" Tell me more...")

Some interviewers are trained to continue to ask probing questions after the candidate has given an initial response; in fact, this probing technique is a well-established component of behavioral interviewing, detailed in Chapters 4 and 5. In his blog directed at hiring decision-makers, Better Hiring Today, Adam Robinson, recommends asking "Tell me more" follow-ups three times for each question because these probing queries, "yield the real substance of the interview." [*http://betterhiringtoday.com/2008/10/01/how-to-conduct-an-interview-part-1/*]

"First, the executive needs to understand the purpose of those probing questions," advises interview coach Georgia Adamson. For example, Adamson suggests predicting where the interviewer is headed when he or she asks the interviewee to dig deeper, as well as what the interviewer hopes to learn from in-depth explorations of a given topic. "The questions can either offer an opportunity to reinforce the value-added/ROI message the executive wants to communicate," Adamson notes, "or lead to a misstep by encouraging the executive to reveal too much information or the wrong kind of information, which could sabotage his or her candidacy." If the interviewer seems bent on digging in dangerous territory, Adamson cautions to "be prepared with a quick-thinking response that doesn't suggest reluctance to provide information but rather redirects the line of questioning in a way that presents positive, non-damaging information about the value you can bring to the position and the company."

"Know what your three or four key strengths are and what your brand is," Rosemarin suggests, "because when probed, all your responses should key into them. For example, if you know you are creative, you should have at least three stories that illustrate your creative impact." Harvey, too, supports having examples and stories ready for probing follow-ups. "For example, an interviewer may ask, 'What strengths do you bring to this position?' In response, you might say, 'I'm results-driven, highly organized, and efficient,'" Harvey suggests. The interviewer will likely ask for substantiation, and "you need to be ready to give examples that demonstrate effectively that you have the strengths that you claim to have," Harvey says. "Your example needs to show clearly how you utilized the strengths of being results-driven, highly organized, and efficient on the job."

Master Career Counselor Sharon McCormick encourages candidates to focus on "the top challenges throughout their career that demonstrate insight into their character and competencies while answering the question." McCormick suggests candidates provide background information into situations that outline their job goals in a specific example that includes "the resources they were given to work with, their decision-making process in approaching the goals, and what results they achieved." She notes that "results need to be quite concrete and understandable to a wide audience."

For a probing followup such as, "Tell me more about your problem-solving approach and ability to get results," McCormick recommends a response like this:

In 2007, I faced a massive reduction in force at our company. I was losing 5,000 people out of a total workforce of 10,000. Now every employee's workload would double, and people would have to be let go that had been with the company for 25 years. I would have no funds to hire interns or temp staff. My approach was to rework our entire operational plan and preserve jobs while cutting costs, which was the real need. I championed my approach to cut costs, which was to limit our suppliers to 10 instead of 30, and I explained my plan and got the backing of our suppliers. I renegotiated costs with those 10 suppliers and signed longer contracts with them, saving millions. Next, I offered flex-time and telecommuting opportunities, which 4,000 employees selected as their work option, also saving millions of dollars. I motivated employees to generate cost savings, and they created more efficient work processes, which saved thousands of dollars. I offered attractive buyout options for 1,000 workers, and every one of them accepted the buy-out.

I was able to keep 9,000 employees and still cut costs. My leadership style is very proactive and focused on helping my people while getting bottom-line results for the company. That is why I have a reputation as a caring leader. My region continues to be the most profitable and my turnover is the lowest.

In fact, executive interviewees need to have ready multiple stories like this one for use when the interviewer probes for more information. Career coach Robyn Feldberg suggests choosing stories that "demonstrate your personal brand, unique promise of value, and the major competencies that the prospective employer will be likely to look for given the nature and demands of the position."

Making the case for career, job, or industry transition

Let's face it; given the choice of hiring someone with strong experience in the employer's industry or employing a candidate who is transitioning from a different sector, the hiring decision-maker is much more likely to go with the industry veteran. But the savvy executive can convince the employer to take a leap of faith. "The key to making the move successfully is to not only inventory your own skills, but to package them so they're appropriate for the industry you're targeting," Harvey advises. "Understanding an industry isn't difficult but does require research, whether that means reading reports on the industry from the Bureau of Labor Statistics or taking a contact from that industry out to lunch to pick his or her brain," Harvey says. She notes that employers don't want a long learning curve. "They want someone who can speak the lingo and hit the ground running," Harvey states. "The trick is to convince them that you can contribute right away. So read trade journals, talk to insiders, and get a really good handle on what's going on in that industry and in that company in particular."

Rosemarin agrees that you, as a transitioning executive, should learn as much as possible about your prospective new space. "I see it as two islands when it comes to industry shifting," she says. "You are on one island, and the other industry is on the other island. What you need to do is learn the ways of those on the other island and then build a 'translation bridge' between the two so that those on the other side can understand how what you have been doing and your expertise is not as alien as they might have originally surmised."

Feldberg notes that "business is business, regardless of industry." She advises candidates to "make sure you project the confidence, competence, aptitude, and personal drive the employer needs, and demonstrate proof of performance meeting new challenges."

"Transitioning to a new career, job, or industry requires that you convince an employer during the interview that you have knowledge of the field or industry in combination with essential transferrable skills," Finkle observes. "Examples such as attending professional meetings or conferences in the field, contacting industry leaders, and conducting extensive informational interviews with professionals in the career area demonstrate your effort and initiative to learn as much as possible about the profession and industry," she says. Finkle cites the importance during the interview to connecting your new knowledge "with the skills and experience that you have acquired and how this powerful combination makes you a strong candidate. For example, if you have extensive experience in marketing, and you are interested in working with social entrepreneurs, highlight your knowledge of current trends in the field, why businesses with a social conscience support your values and how your marketing talents could contribute to the successful launch of this new business."

"During the interview, demonstrate a thorough knowledge and understanding of the industry trends, issues, and challenges," Harvey suggests. "Explain what problems you have solved and what solutions you have delivered that can be applied to this industry; and clearly define the value you can bring to the organization," she offers.

Working with recruiters in the interview process

As noted in Chapter 1, working with recruiters at the executive and senior levels is quite common. Recruiters themselves may interview you, and they will likely also work with you extensively to prepare you for interviews with their client employers and debrief you after the interviews. Epstein, who has been an executive recruiter for more than a dozen years, notes that in many cases, recruiters are the first to interview a candidate. Some recruiters will interview candidates even when they do not have a specific search assignment that fits the candidate, while others interview individuals only for a particular open search. In an initial interview with a recruiter who is trying to fill a search assignment that fits you, "your job is to help the recruiter understand what value you can bring to the company and that you are more than what they ever dreamed of," Rosemarin says. Your interviewing behavior with the recruiter will tell him or her a great deal about how well you will interview with the client employer, so take this interview just as seriously as you would an interview directly with the hiring employer. Before the recruiter interview, the candidate pool is bigger than it will be after the recruiter interviews candidates for a given job. Some candidates will be screened out and never even get to interview with the employer. Interview well so that the screened-out candidate won't be you.

Typically, executive recruiters will do everything they can to ensure that qualified candidates they are working with get and accept the employer's job offer. That's why recruiters like Epstein encourage candidates to be honest with them. "Make sure you tell the recruiter everything he or she might need to know," Epstein advises. "Surprises only hurt you later on." Build a trusting relationship with your recruiter." Maureen Mack, a human resources consultant with H.R. Principal, LLC, in Walnut Creek, Calif, agrees. "The more they know, they more they can help you and determine if you are a fit for their client," she says, adding that a recruiter who decides that you are not a fit for that assignment might know of a different position that you would fit.

Epstein also recommends that candidates practice interviewing with the recruiter so they are prepared before the real interview. Mack notes that once a recruiter determines whether the candidate possesses appropriate skills for a given job, he or she can offer interview coaching. "For example, I am a pretty casual person, and my sense of humor pops out in almost every conversation," Mack says. "That can be a detriment during the interview process. A recruiter might tell me that he or she thinks I would be good fit for the hiring manager, but I will need to be serious to get through all the interviews."

Positioning yourself for a volatile economy

"When the economy is uncertain, you shouldn't be," writes Dave Opton, founder and CEO of ExecuNet. [downloadable from *http://www. execunet.com/executive-jobs-report.cfm*]. Candidates will need to consider "the somewhat extraordinary challenges and pressures the company is likely to be facing in today's business environment," Adamson advises. "Then they need to identify and appropriately frame ways in which they can help the company overcome those challenges." Intense research is critical, Adamson says, because candidates "must demonstrate a comprehensive grasp of the challenges and their unique qualifications and attributes that will enable them to build and maintain forward momentum under the extreme conditions the company is probably experiencing." Candidates also need to be alert to positive opportunities as well. "If a company actually sees some favorable possibilities in the current environment," Adamson says, "the executive who hopes to work there must be able to communicate his or her ability to capitalize on those possibilities and make the most of them."

Especially in a troubled economy, the hiring decision-maker is worried about making the wrong hiring decision, notes Rosemarin. "Be able to take care of the interviewer's anxiety. Tell a story that illustrates your strengths and value—which is your brand—to assure the interviewer that you will take care of his or her worries," she says.

Harvey suggests that candidates highlight accomplishments related to "keeping a company afloat or thriving during a difficult time." While the global recession that began in 2008 was virtually unprecedented, Harvey notes that candidates can still cite their leadership in getting past market downturns, slumps, or crises. "As a senior executive, explain how you keep threatened companies afloat and how you position them as industry leaders despite economic crisis," Harvey recommends. "Explain the most difficult times the company experienced and showcase your contributions to the company's survival."

After the Interview: Thank-yous, Follow-up, References, Vetting, and Background Checks

At the senior and executive levels, the activity that takes place after the interview—or after a series of interviews—is critical for both candidate and employer. You as the candidate should be concerned with analyzing your performance and extending the courtesy of thanking your interviewers in a way that bolsters your candidacy. Then, continue to follow up to show your interest. Meanwhile, the employer will be checking your references, and later at the offer stage, probably vetting you through a background check. This chapter guides you through these activities.

Post-mortem: Analyzing your performance after the interview

Is there any point in reliving a job interview you've just gone on? Can any good come from analyzing it and ruminating on it? While it's tempting to feel that there's no reason to cry over spilled milk, conducting a post-mortem exam on your interview serves at least two purposes:

1. The analysis of what went right and what went wrong will help you structure your thank-you letter. However, since the thank-you letter should be sent quickly after the interview, you may need to abbreviate your initial analysis of the interview and conduct a more in-depth post-mortem after you've sent out your thank-yous.

2. Your review of the interview will help you in your next interview. First thing to do—just as soon after the interview as you can—is to jot down everything you remember about the interview, especially the content. Write down all the questions you remember being asked. Take some notes on how you responded to each question. Do you identify any information that you forgot to mention in your responses? Did you say anything you wish you hadn't said? Did any of your responses seem weak? You may want to revisit these content areas when you write your thank-you letter.

The next critical thing to ask yourself is how good was the chemistry or rapport between you and the interviewer? If you were not able to build rapport in the interview, you may not be able to salvage your chances. But you can try in your follow-ups.

If you write your thank-you letter with a tone of warmth and mention how much you enjoyed talking with the interviewer, you may pull off the psychological trick of convincing the interviewer that rapport actually was strong between the two of you. Try to recall any personal interests the interviewer mentioned during the small-talk portions of the interview. If the interviewer gave you nothing verbally to latch onto, perhaps his or her office indicated personal interests. Did you spot any collectibles in the office? The point is, try to strike a chord with the interviewer by bringing up topics that show that you paid attention to his or her personality. For example:

o "How 'bout those Mets?"

o "I loved your collection of glass figurines. Have you visited that new shop on 6th Street? They have a wonderful selection there."

o "After you mentioned that article on branding in *Business Week*, I read it myself, and I agree with you about the impact these concepts will have in our industry."

Next, recall the interviewer's response to your answers to his or her questions. Can you distinguish the answers that seemed to be home-runs based on the interviewer's reaction? For example, did the interviewer's eyes light up, did he or she smile or nod during any of your responses? Did you detect a look of concern or a lack of connection during other responses? Your home-run responses are the ones to emphasize in your thank-you letter.

The responses you gave that did not seem to elicit a positive response from the interviewer could be targets for damage control in your thank-you letter. Damage control must be considered extremely carefully and handled cautiously because you don't want to bring up negatives. An interview response you thought was weak might have seemed perfectly fine to the interviewer, so you don't want to call attention to it or blow it up into something big when the interviewer may have found the flaw inconsequential. Save damage control for situations in which you gave an off-base or incomplete response. Instead of being negative or apologetic in your thank-you letter, simply state that you would like to give a more complete answer to the question, and then do so.

Now, reflect on what the interviewer really emphasized during your meeting. Finish this sentence: "Based on what the interviewer stressed in this interview, the most significant need I could fill for the employer is _____." In your thank-you letter, demonstrate that you picked up on that need, you understand it, and you are ready to fill it. The interviewer's emphasis can also serve as a guide to what to leave out of your letter. You may have gone into the interview convinced of the importance of mentioning particular skills or accomplishments, but if the interviewer's emphasis was in other areas, you probably have no need to bring them up in your letter.

Did the interviewer voice any concerns about your qualifications? Did he or she raise any objections? If you didn't address these in the interview, confront them in your thank-you letter. And be sure in your next interview to ask whether the interviewer has any concerns about hiring you.

Did you ask all the questions you intended to when the interviewer opened up the discussion for your queries? If not, consider asking one or two in your thank-you.

How did the interview close? What next steps did the interviewer describe? Be sure you understand the process and reinforce your understanding in your letter; doing so will help propel the next step into action. If you aren't sure of the next step, try to find out, perhaps through a quick e-mail to the interviewer or a call to his or her assistant. (And if you didn't find out in the interview what the next step is, keep in mind for future interviews to always ask about the decision process at the end of the meeting.)

Finally, what is your overall gut feeling about the interview? Sometimes we walk out of a job interview absolutely confident we aced it; other times, we're pretty sure we blew it. It's important to check in with how well you performed, measure that feeling against the hiring outcome, and diagnose what went right or wrong with the interview. For example, if you felt your performance was stellar, but you don't get the job offer or at least move on to the next step in the hiring process, your perceptions about your interview skills may be off base. You may want to do some mock interviews with friends or career practitioners to get their feedback. Of course, it's quite possible that your performance was indeed stellar, but the employer found someone else to be a better fit with the job. If you don't get the offer, you can try asking the interviewer to critique your interview; however, most employers these days won't provide such feedback as they fear lawsuits. If you have a network contact inside the organization, you may be able to get feedback through that person.

While it's sometimes uncomfortable or even painful to relive a job interview, performing an autopsy on it is important to enable you to follow up effectively and to determine what you can do differently in your next interview. For example, are there recurring questions or topics that seem to cause you difficulty in interviews? Plan to polish those areas for future interviews. To conduct a truly comprehensive post-mortem of your interview, use the Post-Mortem Survey at http://www.quintcareers.com/interview_post-mortem.pdf. Don't forget to consult the survey before your next interview.

Thanking your interviewer

"The biggest mistake that interviewees make is not following up with vigor and enthusiasm," says Judy Rosemarin, president of Sense-Able Strategies, Inc., New York City. The first step in this follow-up process is a thank-you letter or note, and the most significant reason to send one is that it is simply common courtesy to thank people for their time and attention. "It is an absolute must to show interest in the position and appreciation for the time spent during the interview," says Robert Shotton, chair at the Society of Manufacturing Engineers in Hamilton, Ontario, Canada. While a shocking number of job-seekers at lower levels omit this act of good manners, senior-level candidates and executives have a better track record. Chuck Matthews, corporate director, human resources at G&T Conveyor in Tavares, FL, says he gets thank-yous from executives about 85 percent of the time.

A thank-you letter is another opportunity to demonstrate your communication skills. As Jeremy Shapiro, senior vice president at Hodes iQ, New York City, notes, "thank-you notes are one of the few unsolicited writing samples a manager receives." As such, of course, you'll want to ensure that your letter reads well and is free of grammatical errors, misspellings, or typos.

Good etiquette is far from the only reason to send a thank-you. With a well-crafted thank-you letter, you can restate your enthusiasm for the job and organization, demonstrate your understanding of the position, and emphasize the match between you and the job, as well as how you mesh with the company culture, especially now that you know more about it having experienced the interview.

You can also suggest what your immediate contributions could be if you are selected for the position. "Use the letter as a forum to address current issues the employer is facing and propose solutions," recommends Barb Poole, president of Hire Imaging, LLC. "You're contributing to the employer's success even before coming on board! Turn the thank-you into a self-marketing tool that validates your candidacy, builds rapport and reminds the reader of your value."

In their book *For Executives Only: Applying Business Techniques to Your Job Search*, Bill Belknap and Helene Seiler suggest that the letter sent after an interview is a prime opportunity to influence the hiring decision-maker. The content, the authors write, needs to focus on the organization's key business issues "and how you can best influence them."

"The candidate's ability to quickly digest the tenor of the interview, and the managers who they'll be working with is an early indicator of success,"

Shapiro says. Poole agrees: "It's critical that the executive candidate reminds prospective employers of their interest and fit. The thank-you is the perfect vehicle for communicating this, allowing you to sell your strengths again. Maximize the thank-you letter's strategic purpose to repackage your skills and accomplishments in another format—and market your value."

A good argument for writing the letter immediately after the interview is that you'll recall the interview more clearly, especially the points that the interviewer seemed especially interested in. "I always like to tell my clients to 'velcro back' to the actual interview and refer back to the places that you both agreed upon or with what you were most intrigued," Rosemarin says. Build on these high points and the strengths of the interview in your letter.

Bring up anything you thought of after the interview that is pertinent to the employer's concerns. "You will often think of things post-interview that you could have said during the meeting," Poole says. If you left important information out of any of your responses, it's fine to add that information in your letter: "I meant to mention that my project-management skills have saved my current employer significant costs."

The letter is also an opportunity to expand on responses you gave. If, for example, the interviewer told you exactly what the company was looking for in a candidate, you probably explained how you meet that description. But with further reflection after the interview, you can describe more fully how you fit the profile.

As mentioned on page 167, damage control in a thank-you note is possible if handled carefully. You can also speak to any objections you sense the employer may have to hiring you, but again you must be careful not emphasize or introduce negatives that weren't there in the first place.

Your thank-you letter can be a vehicle for indicating that you are providing additional materials (such as references) that the interviewer has requested or that you feel might positively affect the hiring decision.

A final important role for the thank-you letter is to restate your understanding of the next step in the process. Given the multi-interview hiring process, asking in each interview about the next step and mentioning it in your thank-you letter will provide a small psychological prompt for the reader.

Most hiring decision-makers interviewed for this book indicated that an e-mailed thank-you is sufficient, but a typed business letter is a nice touch, and some hiring decision-makers even expressed a preference for a handwritten message on a notecard. Handwritten notes are seen rarely enough to get noticed when they're sent. Research suggests that taking the action to thank the interviewer is far more important than the form that action takes. To be sure the hiring manager gets your thank-you quickly but you also employ an appealing level of formality, e-mail your thank-you within 24 hours of the interview, but follow it up with a hard-copy version, whether typed or handwritten.

As we saw in Chapter 4, it's a virtual certainty that your executive interview process will entail multiple interviews and numerous people. Send a thank-you to each person. Ideally you will have collected each person's business card at the interview, but if you did not, call each person's assistant to ensure you have correct titles and names—including spellings—of all the people who interviewed you. You can use a boilerplate letter as a template, but vary at least a sentence or two to individualize the letters in case your recipients compare notes. And here's an idea that will set you apart: Send a thank-you to the hiring manager's assistant and any other support staffers who helped make arrangements for your interviews. These unsung heroes rarely get thank-you notes; yours will endear you to them.

Will a thank-you make or break your candidacy? Why take the risk? Dawn Boyer, director of marketing, sales, public relations and human resources for MonsterClean in Virginia Beach, Va., for example, so disdains candidates who are "so arrogant that they don't believe basic protocol or common courtesy should be followed," that she believes "they shouldn't be considered for the position if there is an equally qualified and more gracious candidate available."

"I keep score," says Matthews. "Those who send follow-up letters demonstrate their professional courtesy and attention to detail. This factor has made a difference regarding candidate selection." For Anders Mikkelson, managing director at Berlin Pacific, New York City, the lack of a thank-you not only shows lack of interest but a missed "opportunity to emphasize talking points." Shapiro says he's pretty sure that "100 percent of those that were hired sent one." Sending a thank-you, Shapiro observes, is "certainly related to key attributes most companies are looking for in senior talent." For some employers, the lack of a thank-you letter is not enough to eliminate a candidate, but if the decision-maker has reservations about the candidate, the failure to send a thank-you note can be the nail in the coffin because it shows inattention to detail, lack of courtesy, and poor follow-up skills.

Identifying and prepping your references

If you're like most job-seekers, you may not have put much thought into whom you'll want to use as references when potential employers request them. We're often so busy polishing our resumes and cover letters, researching employers, and preparing for interviews, that we neglect a very important part of the job-search process—requesting people to be references.

Do not underestimate the power of your references. Remember, the employer is preparing to make a big investment in hiring you and wants to be sure you are who you say you are. Having a few good references can be the deciding factor in your getting the job offer. Similarly, having one negative—or lukewarm—reference could cost you the job.

Think strategically about reference choices. You want about three to five references who will make the strongest recommendations for you. "Acquire a cadre of references from whom you can select to customize your response to a reference request from a specific prospective employer," advises career counselor Susan Gaurneri, who recommends relevant references from current and former supervisors; colleagues and peers; members of boards of directors; strategic partner companies, and government agencies; key customers; professional association and community leaders; vendors and consultants; and those whom you have mentored who have become leaders in your field. You may not always have free choice in the references you choose, as an employer or recruiter you are working with may ask you to submit certain kinds of references. Some employers don't consider colleagues and co-workers to be valuable references.

"A professional reference can speak about your performance on the job," says professional executive career coach Don Orlando, owner of The McLean Group, Montgomery, Ala. For that reason, Orlando advises using friends or members of the clergy only as a last resort. "They cannot give employers much of the information they need to decide if you should be interviewed or hired," Orlando notes.

It is not mandatory to include all former supervisors as references, especially if they did not know all your accomplishments, or you fear they will not have glowing things to say about you. Sometimes former co-workers, or supervisors in other departments who know your work, make the best choices. Again, the key is people who know your strengths and abilities—and who will say positive things about you.

Be aware also that employers, especially at the executive level, often conduct informal reference checking through members of their network, so you likely won't have complete control over who speaks for you.

Obviously, you need permission to use anyone as a reference; be sure to ask each if each prospective reference is comfortable serving in that role for you. Most people will be flattered—or at least willing to serve as a reference—but ask to be sure. Some may decline your request.

Educate and coach your references. Ensure that each reference has a copy of your most current resume, knows your key accomplishments and skills, and is aware of the positions you seek. The best references know who you are, what you can accomplish, and what you want to do. "Executives must spend time maintaining and improving their relationships with their references," advises Randall M. Craig, president of Pinetree Advisors Inc., in Toronto. "When it is time to use them, prepared candidates should provide details of the new position, reminders from their time working together, and any other important details.

Guarneri suggests keeping references informed by including them in your LinkedIn network and asking them to contribute to LinkedIn recommendations. After each interview, alert your references that they may be getting a phone call from the employer.

Collect all the details for each reference. Complete information from each reference is mandatory. Orlando recommends gathering the following information:

- o Full name and courtesy title, such as Colonel, Dr., Professor, Judge
- o Phonetic pronunciation of the reference's name (if it's difficult to pronounce). For example: "Sienkiewicz" is pronounced "sin-cavage."
- o Job title

- o Organization's name
- o Full business mailing address (try to avoid post office boxes) including ZIP
- o Daytime phone number, including area code and the best time to call, as well as cell phone number
- o Private e-mail address
- o Reference's professional relationship to you (former supervisor, colleague, customer, vendor, supplier, pro-bono client, volunteer committee member, and the like) and the number of years you have known each other professionally.

On your references list, Guarneri suggests, "provide links to your references' LinkedIn Profiles, blogs, and company Websites as well." Orlando adds, "you may improve your chances greatly if you have a powerful LinkedIn page, particularly if your page includes recommendations and endorsements. Gaurneri advises asking each reference to supply a brief listing of your top three to four strengths and accomplishments that demonstrate your branded value proposition.

Be aware of questions employers typically ask of references. That knowledge not only will help you coach your references, but will also help you to speak preemptively in the interview if you know the answers to any of these questions are sticky issues for you.

In addition to asking for substantiation of claims you've made about yourself, an employer or recruiter might ask the following questions of your references. * Denotes a question contributed by Adam Robinson, founder and CEO of the Ionix Hiring Systems. Reprinted with permission:

- o Can you please describe how you know the candidate? And for how long?
- o How would you rate the candidate's skills in _____?
- o Can you describe the candidate's communications abilities?
- o How well does the candidate work under pressure?
- o How well does the candidate take constructive criticism?
- o How well does the candidate interact with co-workers?
- o Is the candidate a team player?
- o How would you describe the candidate's honesty and integrity?

- How receptive is the candidate to new ideas and procedures?
- Can you describe the candidate's leadership, managerial, or supervisory skills?
- *What are the candidate's strengths, in your opinion? You know, things that really stand out, things that you like and respect about him/her.
- *What would you consider to be the candidate's biggest areas for improvement?
- *What areas of performance are [candidate]'s weakest?
- *Let's talk about the candidate's job duties while working for you. Could you clarify for me what [candidate]'s responsibilities were when working for you?
- *What metrics did you use to measure the candidate's performance?
- *On a scale of 1-10, with 10 being "outstanding," how would you rate [candidate]'s overall performance?
- *Can you confirm for me how [candidate]'s compensation was structured?
- *What was the starting and ending salary for [candidate]?
- *Let me tell you about the job I am considering hiring [candidate] for. [Describe job]. Based on your experience with [candidate], how do you think he/she might perform in that role? Do you think that this role is a stretch for him/her?
- *Is there anything that you've observed about your time managing [candidate] that I should be aware of, good or bad?
- *What's the best advice you can give me for how I can best manage [candidate]?
- *Is there anything else about [candidate] that you feel is important for my overall evaluation of their fit for my open position?
- *If, given the opportunity to hire [candidate] again for a similar job, would you enthusiastically rehire him/her?

Tom Adam, a senior contract recruiter in Los Angeles, focuses on contributions and innovations when talking with a candidate's references. "Candidates for senior or executive positions will be expected, if hired, to bring about innovative and productive changes to an organization; they are not being hired to simply maintain the status quo," Adam says. He asks references about improvements candidates were asked to make and the needed improvements they uncovered above and beyond their original mandate. These improvements beyond the executive's mandate are, Adam notes, "what can separate the good candidate from the great candidate. Asking references about such contributions can yield very valuable information."

Be sure to thank your references once your current job search is complete. These people were willing to help you, and thanking them is simply good manners.

If you learn that a negative reference has derailed your candidacy, try to find out what was said so you can avoid future fiascos. In her book, *Job Search Debugged*, Rita Ashley suggests using this wording with the employer: "I am at a loss to figure out what might have been said to take me out of the running in this job. I appreciate you cannot disclose who you talked to, but in order for me to continue my job search, it would help to know what was said so I can offset the concern for future employers. Will you help?"

Here are a few "don't's" in the references realm: Don't list names of references on your resume. References belong on a separate sheet of paper that matches the branded look and feel of your resume, but is titled "References," "Reference List," or "References Dossier." Don't offer references to employers until the employer requests them, but do be sure to keep a list of references with you when interviewing so that you can be prepared to present them when the interviewer asks. If you have a career portfolio, keep the list in your portfolio. Don't bother with letters of recommendations. Employers don't want to read letters written in the past to "whom it may concern." Employers want to be able to contact and communicate (via phone or e-mail) with a select group of people who can speak about your strengths and weakness and fit for the job you are seeking. Letters of recommendation also lack credibility because anyone who would write a letter for you would likely say only good things about you.

If you are really unsure of what your references will say about you, you have the option of hiring a job reference service. For a fee, the company will contact each of your references and report back to you what they said about you. Ideally, though, you should not need to use these services. See services listed in the Appendix B.

Minimizing skeletons during vetting and background checks

The words of Jay Meschke, president of CBIZ Executive Search, Kansas City, Mo., capture the prevailing philosophy about background checks in the executive job search: "For executives, background checks are so routine in the recruitment process that one would need to question the sanity of the hiring entity that does not perform background checks in this day and age." Resume and credential fraud, Meschke notes, have contributed to a dramatic increase in background checks. Nick Fishman, chief marketing officer and executive vice president for employeescreenIQ in Cleveland, Ohio, notes that his firm "finds a 56 percent discrepancy rate between what candidates claim about their past employment and academic credentials and what we find when we inquire." Employers also conduct background searches to guard against lawsuits filed claiming company liability when an employee causes harm that better vetting might have prevented (because the check probably would have prevented the individual from being hired and causing the alleged harm).

An employer, or more likely, a third-party firm that specializes in background checks, may scrutinize a wide variety of elements in the background-checking process, including federal, state and local criminal proceedings and convictions; federal, state and local civil litigation, bankruptcy court records, magistrate's court records, U.S. tax court records, federal and state tax liens and warrants, surrogate and probate court records, matrimonial and family court records, judgment indices, pending suits, UCC filings, mechanics liens, property records, educational verification, prior employment, corporate/partnership filings and entity filings, fictitious business name indices; regulatory checks including, SEC filings, FINRA (Financial Industry Regulatory Authority) records/actions, CFTC (Commodity Futures Trading Commission) records, arbitration records; Department of Motor Vehicles records; professional registration and licensing; local, national, international Internet/media review; general interest, trade, and limited access publications; business databases, including general information, business relationships, and records of stock ownership;

federal agencies, including, EPA, FTC, FCC, EEOC, Department of Energy, Federal Home Loan Bank Board, Federal Election Commission; state agencies, including secretary of state, attorney general, casino control, consumer affairs, environmental; and local sources, including city agencies, Better Business Bureau, local law enforcement; reputation inquiries with former employees, associates, employers, and industry sources.

In this vetting process, the employer or investigator attempts to identify misrepresentations or omissions, unreported financial difficulties, illegal or unethical business practices, undisclosed legal proceedings, criminal or regulatory actions, sanctions, debarments or de-listings, and troubled transactional histories.

The issues for candidates include how to prepare for background checks and how to handle them. Experts from background-checking and related firms explain.

Know the red flags in your own background. "Assume that every detail of your background will be uncovered, because it probably will," says Maureen Mack, human-resources consultant with H.R. Principal, LLC in Walnut Creek, Calif. Several background-check experts advise paying a service to conduct a background check on yourself before you begin interviewing so you know what an employer might find (see services listed in Appendix B). As Craig points out, this process may reveal situations in which someone who shares your name has an unsavory background. While Craig says you can do nothing about this person's red flags, you can let the hiring decision-maker know that while a background check may reveal an issue, the person named is not actually you.

Chris Fabrycki, who worked in corporate functions for years as an executive recruiter and is now owner and HR consultant with Accent Services, LLC, in Warren, N.J., notes that because a significant aspect of the vetting process involves a financial check, ordering a credit check on yourself can help. "I have seen many senior-level finalist candidates with bad credit, which can prompt a stop to the hiring process," she says. The information you'll turn up in a credit check is limited, however, so Fabrycki agrees with the many experts who recommend investing the money in using a reliable company to conduct your own full background check.

Craig also recommends conducting a search for yourself on Google and social media sites (Facebook, LinkedIn, and similar social and networking sites) and remove any questionable content that you can control. Statistics from ExecuNet's study, "Dealing With Your Digital Dirt 3.0," indicate that an overwhelming majority (86 percent) of executive recruiters conduct online searches as part of their background checking, and, as a result, nearly half (44 percent) of these recruiters have eliminated candidates because of something questionable they uncovered. [*http://members.execunet.com/promo/pdf/ ExecuNet_A_CareerGuide_DIGITAL_DIRT_VERSION3.0_2008.pdf*] Craig advises setting up a Google e-mail alert for your name so you receive notification every time you are mentioned online.

Eliminate any issues you can. "For a no-surprise background check, the executive should resolve any outstanding disputes or pending items," Craig suggests, noting that reviewing credit reports for discrepancies and ensuring that any legal actions are settled are solid steps toward eliminating troublesome skeletons.

Be scrupulously honest in any paperwork you submit during the interview process. While some executives may feel that completing an employment application is beneath them, many employers require applications for legal reasons. Every background-check expert interviewed for this book emphasized honesty in applications or any other paperwork you are asked to submit as part of the hiring procedure. Mack recalls having to terminate "a really good guy because he lied about something in his background." Mack explains that the issue came up in the background check a few months into his employment (because background checks took longer at that time). Mack says her company would have hired him even if they knew about it, "but we terminated him because he lied on his employment application."

Understand the value of pre-emptive disclosure, recommends Craig. "If there is a 'red flag,' then it is better to disclose it during the interview process, where the issue can be put into context," Craig advises. "Discovering it by surprise in a background check will usually lead to a disqualification." On the flip side, "many employers will not have an issue with a [problem disclosed during the check] as long as they feel it has no impact on the position," Fabrycki notes. "I would advise candidates to tell the employer prior to the first on-site interview; no sense wasting anyone's time if that employer will have a problem," Fabrycki says. "Take your chances with the truth," Mack advises. "If they are checking your background, they already want you as a candidate and will probably work with you," she says. "But if you are hiding info, and they find out, you're toast." Poole points out that this proactive approach can differentiate you from other candidates. "It can also give the recruiter or hiring manager a higher comfort level with you as a candidate, because they know that a reputable company has been retained to certify your credentials and information up front—a potential big leap in gaining an air of integrity and credibility," Poole says.

Know your rights and protect your security. "The first thing to know is that an employer must obtain your consent before performing a background check," Fishman says, noting that the employer also must divulge what the background check consists of. "If an employer chooses not to extend an offer based on the outcome of the search," Fishman explains "it must notify the candidate of this decision, provide him or her with a copy of the report, and allow him or her the opportunity to dispute the findings." Fishman also cautions applicants to be wary when employers ask for the candidate to pay for the background check, particularly over the Internet. "There have been a number of recent scams in this regard," Fishman says.

Meschke advises candidates to ask how the information is transmitted from party to party—vendor to employer. "Assure that the information is encrypted and that Social Security numbers are blacked out in the event the data ends up in the wrong hands," Meschke cautions.

Watch for inaccuracies. A particular value in ordering your own background search is that you may uncover and correct information that is inaccurately reported. "Reporting jurisdictions, municipalities, and credit bureaus are not infallible," Meschke notes. "Mistakes are made. Incorrect information may end up in a person's report due to transposing numbers or using a wrong middle initial in a name search."

"The information found in a search is only as good as the person who entered it," agrees Sandy Glover, president of Gold Shield Legal Investigations, Inc., Ormond Beach, Fla. Glover personally contacts the clerk of the court or makes other personal inquiries if the accuracy of a report is questioned.

Remain calm and relaxed during the process, advises Certified Protection Professional Philip Farina, CEO of Farina and Associates, Ltd., San Antonio, TX. "Whatever comes up from a pre-employment screening, focus the selection committee toward the positive attributes that you bring to the table. All things being equal, the employment candidate who checks out quickly and accurately may get the position," Farina says.

Following up

Everything in this chapter to this point reinforces the idea that your work is far from done once you finish the interview. Be proactive and consider follow-up a strategic part of your job-search process. Follow-up can give you the edge you need to get the job offer over others who interviewed for the position. Since the senior- and executive-level interview process virtually always involves multiple interviews, your goal in following up—until you know you've undergone the final interview—is to get to the next step in the process. If you are working with a recruiter, you can follow up with that professional and depend on him or her to follow up with the employer.

As we saw in Chapter 5, part of your interview closing is to ask the interviewer the next step in the process and when he or she expects to make the decision regarding whether you will move forward. Based on the timeline offered in response to your question, follow up with a telephone call or e-mail to the employer at the appropriate time to ask about the position. Take another opportunity to build rapport and sell your strengths during this communication.

Continue to follow up, especially if the employer asks you to, until you've achieved the next step in the process or learn you've been eliminated. Just don't go overboard and annoy or bother the employer. One trick is to do some of your follow-up by calling after hours so you can leave an upbeat voicemail. That way the decision-maker knows you're interested and following up but doesn't have to be interrupted to interact with you. You can also employ letters and e-mails in your follow-up efforts. Be patient with an executive hiring process that will likely take longer than you or the employer expect. Keep the employer or recruiter informed of any other offers you receive, or of course, if you accept another offer.

If you've done as much follow-up as you can without being annoying, but are not hearing anything, check with members of your network who are inside the organization or have connections there to see what you can learn about how the hiring process is going and solicit their thoughts on what your next steps should be.

Don't burn bridges if you do not get a job offer. You can often turn a rejection into a positive by bringing interviewers into your network, possibly even asking them for referrals to other contacts.

Weighing and Negotiating the Offer and Compensation Package

Whether you love the art of salary negotiation or dread it, the truth is that knowing negotiation tactics for your total compensation package—and avoiding salary negotiation landmines—are key to obtaining the job offer you seek and deserve. One note about negotiation: If you are working with a recruiter, he or she will answer your questions about the package and help resolve issues; however, most recruiters want to ensure that you will accept the position if offered even before you start interviewing, so they will have already reviewed the likely compensation package with you. It's extremely important to be absolutely open and honest with the recruiter about your compensation history and expectations; in fact, if you are not willing to tell the recruiter your salary, he or she likely will not present you to client employers.

Evaluating and negotiating your job offer and compensation package

Probably the biggest mistake you can make is simply deciding to settle and accept whatever offer you receive. While research shows a large percentage of corporate recruiters are willing to negotiate compensation, only a small percentage of candidates actually do so. Research shows that female candidates often make this mistake—either from not completely understanding the negotiation process or from a dislike or discomfort with the idea of negotiating. Settling for a lower salary than you are worth has some major negative financial consequences—you'll earn less, receive smaller raises (because most raises are based as a percentage of your salary), and have a smaller pension (since pension contributions are usually a percentage of your salary). Settling for an offer that you feel in your heart is too low will not only set you back financially, but also eat at you until you finally begin to seriously dislike your job and/or employer. If you have no intention of accepting the company's offer, however, don't waste your time or the company's by entering into negotiation. Negotiation is a process designed to find common ground between two or more parties. Of course, in certain professions, such as sales, the employer expects you to negotiate your salary. On the other hand, some employers simply will not negotiate, citing a number of factors, such as the strength of the economy, the size and vitality of the company, and the supply of job candidates with similar qualifications.

"Executives have been primed to believe that unless they ask for the moon, they will be leaving money on the table. In reality, it's relatively easy to find out salary data," says Elene Cafasso with Enerpace, Inc., Executive and Personal Coaching. As we've seen in the salary-question material in Chapter 5, information is the key to salary negotiation. With the number and variety of salary resources available online—from salary.com and salaryexpert.com to professional associations and research through your network—there is no excuse for you as the candidate not to know your market value. As also discussed in Chapter 5, you should also have researched your prospective employer's historical salary levels, negotiation policies, performance appraisals before the interview process, and geographic, economic, industry, and company-specific factors that might affect the given salary. Ideally, you will have also used your network to obtain information on the employer's standard benefits package so that you have information beyond salary. Even if you decide not to negotiate salary, you'll have a better understanding of the market for your services—and your value in that market. Know going into the offer phase what you will accept as your minimum compensation package, the number below which you will walk away from negotiations.

Never stop selling yourself throughout the negotiation process. Keep reminding the employer of the impact you will make, the problems you will solve, the revenue you will generate. And continue expressing interest and enthusiasm for the job and the company. If you have clearly demonstrated your value to the organization, you will increase your negotiating power. Avoid entering negotiations with the wrong attitude. Always have in the back of your mind that your goal with these negotiations is a win-win. You want to get a better deal, but you also need to let the employer feel as though the organization got a good deal as well. "It's important for the executive to feel that the boss is reasonable, invested in his or her success and willing to expend some effort to position him or her for success," Cafasso says. "The negotiation process for hiring really lays the groundwork for the executive's and hiring manager's ability to work together moving forward. If this process is painful, the hire probably will not be successful."

Remember that you'll have your greatest negotiation leverage between the time the employer makes the original offer and the time you accept the final offer. Before you have an offer, you really have no basis for negotiation. Once you accept an offer, you have little to no room to negotiate. It's at the offer point when you can ask more specifics about salary, stock options, bonuses, commissions, health insurance, and other perks. Never make demands. Instead, raise questions and make requests during negotiations. Keep the tone conversational, not confrontational.

For Cafasso and her executive clients, a bigger issue than leaving money on the table is a "deprivation vs. abundance mentality." To get at the mentality that will drive negotiations, Cafasso asks her executive clients these questions:

- What do you believe is fair?
- What amount do you really need to earn to not have any resentments or second thoughts about this position?
- What amount is insufficient and you will truly walk away?
- What are the non-cash reasons you want this position?
  Cafasso asks her clients to think about what else they need to

be positioned for success and do their best work. Club
memberships? Executive coaching/onboarding coaching?
Airline clubs? So much vacation? Guaranteed bonus in year
one? Cafasso then tells her clients to:

o   Ask for what you want or you won't get it.

o   Make sure what you ask for are things you *really* want.

Since the executive job-search these days tends to drag for a long period,
when you finally obtain that offer after weeks or months, it's not unusual to
want to accept it right on the spot. Or, conversely you receive an offer for the
job of your dreams, but at a salary below what you had expected. You are still
excited, elated actually, but what you do next could have consequences for
years to come.

Even the best offers should be reviewed when you have clear head—and
without the pressure of your future boss or HR director staring at you. Be sure
to thank the interviewer for the job offer and express your continued interest in
the job and the company, but ask for some time to consider all the details. Most
employers are willing to give you some time to contemplate the job offer—
typically one to two weeks (some career experts suggest asking for up to a
month). If you run across an employer who wants a decision immediately, consider long and hard whether you want to work for such a company. It's when
you get the job offer that you have the most power because the employer has
chosen you, so use that power to be certain it's the job and job offer for you—
and consider negotiating for a better offer. Just remember that whatever amount
of time you ask for is the amount of time you have to make your decision.

Not only do you want time to review the offer yourself, but you may want
to ask others to review it—perhaps a trusted friend, your accountant, an executive or career coach you're working with, a practitioner who specializes in
executive compensation, or your financial adviser. Barb Poole, president of
Hire Imaging, asks her executive clients to consider whether consulting an
attorney specializing in compensation will serve them well. "When there is
something to sign other than a straight list of itemized compensation, it is a
good idea to talk to an attorney before signing," Poole advises, even suggesting that having your attorney negotiate with the attorney for your potential
employer is an option. "Executive packages are complex," Poole says. "As a
top executive, investing in expertise to understand and fully negotiate might be
money well spent." Poole also recommends devoting particular attention to

the "nons," such as noncompete and nondisclosure agreements. "It's a good idea to get legal advice when leaving a good position, relocating, or going to a competitor. What if the new position doesn't work out? Have your attorney explain equity, partnership, bonus, profit-sharing participation, and so on." Poole suggests.

Some candidates reject job offers very quickly when the employer offers a salary much lower than expected. While in many cases you would be justified in rejecting a lowball offer, it's still best to ask for time to consider it before rejecting it outright. If the money is simply far below the average, you may have no choice but to reject the offer. However, if the money is good—but just not as good as you would like—take a closer look at the benefits. A big mistake is declining a job offer too quickly without looking at the entire compensation package. "Because the expectations for the job are often so high with senior-level executives," Poole says, "there is often a great deal of flexibility in terms of salaries, bonuses, golden parachutes, performance clauses, and other perks." For example, some firms that offer lower salaries include larger bonuses or stock options or pay for memberships to exclusive health clubs in their compensation packages. Remember, too, that you should be able to negotiate a handful of the offer's elements to make it even stronger. Author and career coach Rita Ashley tells her clients to *always* negotiate something, no matter how happy they are with the offer. "They are negotiating with their new boss," Ashley points out, "and it sets the tone for how they will work together." Here is a list of items that may be part of a negotiable compensation package:

- o Salary (including raise policies and cost-of-living adjustments)
- o Nonsalary Compensation: signing bonus, performance bonus, profit-sharing, deferred compensation, commission structure, severance package, employee stock ownership plan (ESOP), stock options
- o Relocation Expenses: house-hunting, temporary living allowance, closing costs, travel expenses, spouse job-hunting/re-employment expenses and assistance
- o Benefits: vacation days (number, timing), personal days, sick days, paid holidays, maternity leave, insurance (medical, dental, vision, life, disability), automobile (or other transportation) allowance, expense reimbursement for parking and commuting, 401(k)/retirement benefits, Employee Assistance Program, professional

training/conference attendance, continuing education (tuition reimbursement), professional-association memberships, club (country, health, or athletic) memberships, wellness programs, product discounts, clothing allowance, short-term loans, dependent care, life-partner benefits (vs. spouse-only), technological equipment such as company cell phone, personal digital assistant, or laptop

o Job-specific: frequency of performance reviews (including timing of first review; most experts recommend asking for a review up to six months earlier than the organization typically conducts reviews), timeframe for advancement, job title/role/duties, location/office and office amenities, telecommuting options, work hours and flexibility/flex-time, starting date, decision-making authority, performance standards/goals, reporting relationships, employment contract

If you have a strong interest in the job and the employer is a good fit, but the offer is not what you expected, consider making a counteroffer proposal. If you decide to make a counterproposal, remember that you should only pick just a few elements that you deem most important; you can't negotiate every aspect of the offer. Choose your battles carefully, conduct your research, and write a short counterproposal. If the salary is too low, focus on that aspect in a counteroffer. If you know the firm will not negotiate on salary, focus on modifying a few of the other terms of the offer (such as additional vacation time, earlier performance reviews, signing bonus, relocation expenses).

Negotiate to your strength. If you are a smooth talker (an extravert), call the employer and ask for a follow-up meeting to discuss a counterproposal. If you communicate better in writing, write a counterproposal letter. Whatever you do in this process, always stay professional in handling the negotiations.

Always ask for a higher salary (within acceptable limits) than you are willing to accept so that when the employer counters your proposal, the salary should be near your original goal. And when possible, try to show how your actions (once on board) will recoup the extra amount (or more) that you are seeking—through cost savings or increased sales revenue, productivity, efficiencies.

If the salary you're offered is on the low end—and the employer has stated that salary is not negotiable (probably due to corporate salary ranges or pay-grade levels)—consider negotiating for a signing bonus, higher performance bonuses, or a shorter time frame for a performance review and raise. Always negotiate base salary first, and then move on to other elements of the job offer.

When presenting a counterproposal to the employer, be sure to include a few benefits that are expendable so that you can drop them in a concession to the employer as negotiations continue. Be prepared for any of a number of possible reactions to your counterproposal, from complete acceptance to agreeing to some concessions to refusal to negotiate. Once the employer agrees to your compensation requests, the negotiations are over. You cannot ask for anything more—or you will risk appearing immature or greedy and having the employer's offer withdrawn or rescinded.

While no specific formula exists for writing a successful counterproposal letter, this structure can increase your likelihood of success:

o First Paragraph: Statement of interest and enthusiasm for job/ company; key selling factors. This paragraph is critical in setting up the tone and direction of the negotiations. Be direct and sincere in expressing your interest for the company, thanking the employer for the job offer. Be sure to follow up with your key selling points—how you will make a direct and immediate (or longer-term) impact on the organization.

o Second Paragraph: Negotiating Item No. 1—offer and counterproposal. Restate the particular point from the original offer that you wish to negotiate, followed by your counterproposal— ideally supported through research, a desire to be fairly compensated, or reinforced by the value you will bring to the company.

o Third Paragraph: Negotiating Item No. 2—offer and counterproposal (same strategy as Negotiating Item No. 1)

o Fourth Paragraph: Negotiating Item No. 3—offer and counterproposal (same strategy as Negotiating Item No. 1)

o Fifth Paragraph: Negotiating Item No. 4—offer and counterproposal (same strategy as Negotiating Item No. 1)

o Concluding Paragraph: Conciliatory comments with strong moving-forward statement. Stress that your requests are modest and that your potential impact is great—and that you look forward to accepting the job offer and getting a jump-start on the position as soon as possible.

You can also include paragraphs for items of the original proposal that you completely agree on—doing so makes the letter seem more balanced and that you are not picking apart the entire offer.

You can include paragraphs for any items in the offer that you need clarification or where you are seeking more information, typically for complex issues such as confidentiality and non-compete agreements, or bonus plans.

Be willing to walk away from negotiations. If you don't have a strong position (a good current job or one or more current or potential job offers), you'll find it harder to negotiate. If you really need or want the job, be more careful in your negotiations. If negotiations break down between you and the employer, move on graciously, thanking the employer again for the opportunity—because you never want to burn any bridges. Other alternatives suggested by Bill Belknap and Helene Seiler in their book *For Executives Only* include, instead of accepting or declining, offering to become a consultant for the employer or negotiating a temporary contract.

Once everything is said and done—and you have received a job offer that you find acceptable, be sure you get the final offer in writing. No legitimate employer will have issues with putting the offer in writing, so if yours balks at your request, accuses you of not having any trust, and tries to bully you to accept the verbal agreement, take it as a major red flag that something is seriously wrong. One advantage of writing a counterproposal letter is that you list the terms of the offer in your letter. Also put your job-acceptance in writing. That way, you'll state your understanding of the offer, and the employer can flag any discrepancies in the agreement. Of course, in many cases, you'll be asked to sign an employment contract, which will accomplish the same purpose. Consider having an attorney review the contract, and don't resign from your current position until you've seen the contract, and you and your attorney have scrutinized it.

Choosing from among multiple offers and making the final decision

After much preparation and hard work you have received three job offers. Now you have to decide which is the best offer. Is the best offer always the one paying the highest salary? When comparing job offers, look at all aspects of each job offer. When you also look at each company's benefits package, you might find a very different story, as illustrated in the following table. Benefits can add up to 30 percent to your total compensation.

This example is purely a financial analysis of the three job offers, and does not take into consideration many other important factors that candidates should also evaluate before deciding on a job offer. If you have multiple job offers, don't put the companies into a bidding war for your services; it rarely works out.

	Worldwide Widget, Inc. New York, NY	West Coast Widgets, Inc. Los Angeles, CA	The Widget Company Chicago, IL
Base Salary:	$210,000	$195,000	$185,000
Sign-on Bonus:	$40,000	$35,000	$45,000
Cost of Living Adjustment:	-$31,500	-$20,000	+ $11,000
Stock Options:	$50,000	$10,000	$0
Medical, Dental, Optical:	$6,000	$8,000	$5,000
Life, Disability Insurance:	$3,000	$5,000	$4,000
Company Car/ Driver:	$50,000	$80,000	$50,000

	Worldwide Widget, Inc. New York, NY	West Coast Widgets, Inc. Los Angeles, CA	The Widget Company Chicago, IL
401(K) or Pension Plan:	$20,000	$20,000	$25,000
Severance Package:	$100,000	$120,000	$185,000
Paid Vacation:	$30,000	$24,000	$26,000
Total Compensation Package:	**$477,500**	**$477,000**	**$536,000**

Table contributed by Randall S. Hansen, PhD, founder and CEO of Quintessential Careers.

Whether you are weighing more than one offer or trying to decide whether to accept a single offer, many factors beyond what's in the preceding table will figure into your decision: location if the new position requires you to move; quality of community (including schools and places of worship); the challenge the position provides and your ability to rise to that challenge and excel; the deliverables you will be expected to produce in the position, the opportunities for advancement; your feel for the cultural fit for the organization and whether the environment makes you comfortable and able to do your best work; your rapport with the team you'll be working with and reporting to; the financial health, reputation, and long-term prospects of the organization; the amount of travel expected, as well as other demands on your work-life balance; the organizations' level of social responsibility and commitment to the local community; and more. While ideally you have thoroughly researched the organization before interviewing, you may want to augment your research after receiving an offer, especially tapping into your network to glean insider information on the nitty-gritty character of the employer. If you find it difficult to weigh all the variables that go into your decision, consider consulting with a career practitioner, such as a coach or counselor to help you make your decision.

Appendix A: Executive Interview Checklist

Consult this checklist before you go on your next interview. If you need to refresh your knowledge of any aspect of the checklist, consult the chapter listed for each item.

I have:

___ Thoroughly researched the organization I'm interviewing with, the industry, my interviewer, the position, and my own qualifications and attributes. See Chapter 2.

___ Conducted research so I know all interview logistics, such as parking, office location, paperwork, attire, and the type of interview that will be conducted. I have called to confirm the interview time. See Chapters 3 and 4.

___ Asked for good directions and/or searched for a map/directions from an Internet map site, such as Mapquest, Google Maps, or Yahoo Maps—or decided to use a GPS device. See Chapter 4.

___ Taken a practice run to the location where I'm having the interview–or otherwise ensured I know exactly where it is and how long it takes to get there. See Chapter 4.

___ Prepared and practiced for the interview without memorizing or over-rehearsing my answers. I've reviewed the questions I think I may be asked in the interview, as well as my planned responses to them. I have composed my responses in writing. See Chapter 5.

___ Enlisted a recruiter, career coach, counselor, friend, or family member to conduct a mock interview with me. See Chapter 3.

___ Gotten a good night's sleep. Brushed my teeth and used mouthwash. Bathed or showered. Used deodorant soap and put on deodorant. For confidence, spritzed on a tiny bit of cologne without overdoing it. See Chapter 4.

___ Planned interview attire that is appropriate for the job, the company, and the industry. I have prepared every element of the outfit, including shoes, jewelry, hose, tie, accessories. I have inspected each element carefully. I have ensured that my outfit is clean and neatly pressed. I've checked for spots and removed them. I've checked for rips or tears and sewn them up or chosen another outfit. I've checked for runs in my hose. I've ensured that my shoes are clean and polished. I have a Plan B for attire if I come across any disasters. See Chapter 3.

___ Packed emergency-repair items I might need: small sewing kit, extra pair of pantyhose, spot-remover wipes, tissues, comb and brush, hairspray or gel, makeup for touchups, breath mints, an umbrella, extra copies of my resume, and my career portfolio. See Chapter 3.

I will:

___ Plan to arrive about 10 minutes early since late arrival for a job interview is never excusable. If I'm running late, I'll phone the employer. See Chapter 4.

___ Greet the receptionist or assistant with courtesy and respect and make a good first impression. See Chapter 4.

___ Not chew gum during the interview. See Chapter 3.

___ Bring extra resumes to the interview. See Chapters 3 and 4.

___ Not rely on my resume to do the selling for me; I know I need to sell myself to the interviewer. See Chapter 5.

___ Greet the interviewer with a big smile. I'll confirm the pronunciation of the interviewer(s)' names (if questionable) with the receptionist before going into the interview. See Chapter 3.

___ Shake hands firmly and avoid a limp or clammy handshake. See Chapter 3.

___ Wait until I am offered a chair before sitting. I will be aware of my body language and posture at all times; I will sit upright and look alert and interested at all times. I will avoid fidgeting or slouching. See Chapter 3.

___ Make strong eye contact with the interviewer(s). See Chapter 3.

___ Show enthusiasm about the position and the company. See Chapter 3.

___ Avoid smoking, even if the interviewer does and offers me a cigarette. I'll avoid smoking beforehand so I don't smell like smoke. I will refrain from smoking in my interview attire and isolate this outfit from my clothes that smell like cigarettes. Whether or not I smoke, I will brush my teeth, use mouthwash, or have a breath mint before (not during) the interview. See Chapter 3.

___ Avoid using poor language, slang, and pause words (such as "like," "uh," "you know," and "um"). See Chapter 3.

___ Speak with a strong, forceful voice to project confidence. See Chapter 3.

___ Maintain a high confidence and energy level, but avoid being overly aggressive or cocky. See Chapter 3.

___ Avoid controversial topics. See Chapter 5.

___ Refrain from saying anything negative about former colleagues, supervisors, or employers. See Chapter 5.

___ Ensure that my strong points come across to the interviewer in a factual, sincere manner. See Chapters 3 and 5.

___ Never lie. I will answer questions truthfully, frankly, and succinctly and not over-answer them or ramble aimlessly. See Chapter 5.

___ Stress my achievements and avoid offering any negative information about myself. See Chapter 5.

___ Avoid answering questions with a simple "yes" or "no;" instead, I will explain and give examples. I will describe those things about myself that showcase my talents, skills, and bottom-line value. See Chapter 5.

___ Demonstrate the research I have done on the company and industry when responding to questions. See Chapters 2 and 5.

___ Refrain from bringing up or discussing personal issues or family problems. See Chapters 4 and 5.

___ Remember that the interview is also an important time to evaluate my fit with the interviewer and the employer he or she represents. See Chapter 5.

___ Realize that a short pause before responding to a question to collect my thoughts is okay, but avoid long pauses. Repeating the question aloud or asking for the question to be repeated to buy some thinking time is okay. See Chapter 4.

___ Conduct myself in a way that demonstrates my determination to land the job I am discussing. Avoid closing the door on an opportunity until I am sure about it. See Chapter 5.

___ Refrain from answering cell-phone calls during the interview; in fact, turn my cell phone off (or set to silent ring). See Chapter 3.

___ Show what I can do for the employer rather than demand what the employer can do for me. See Chapter 5.

___ Postpone inquiring about salary, vacations, bonuses, retirement, or other benefits until after I've received an offer. I will be prepared for questions about salary requirements but will try to delay salary talk until I have an offer. See Chapters 5 and 8.

___ Ask intelligent questions about the job, company, or industry, knowing that if I don't ask any questions, I'll indicate a lack of interest. See Chapter 5.

___ Close the interview by telling the interviewer(s) that I am very interested in the job and asking about the next step in the process. See Chapter 5.

___ Request business cards from each person I interviewed with–or at least ask for and jot down the correct spelling of their first and last names. I'll avoid making assumptions about simple names (was it Jon or John?); I'll get the spelling. See Chapter 4.

___ Immediately write down notes after the interview concludes so I don't forget crucial details. See Chapter 7.

___ Analyze my performance to guide my thank-you letters and future interviews. See Chapter 7.

___ Write thank-you letters within 24 hours to each person who interviewed me. I will continue to follow up after the interview. See Chapter 7.

$$\left(\,1\,\right)$$

Appendix B: Resources

Web resources for executives

Job and career portals and networking organizations

Quintessential Careers Job and Career Resources for Executives, Top Managers, and Experienced Mid- and Senior-Level Professionals

http://www.quintcareers.com/executive_jobs.html

Career and job sites that specialize in assisting executives and senior management–and mid-level managers striving for top positions:

6 Figure Jobs
http://www.sixfigurejobs.com
Portal for $100K+ jobs.
hundredK.com
http://hundredK.com
Center for $100K+ job search and recruiting.

futurestep.com
http://www.futurestep.com
A Korn/Ferry company providing outsourced recruitment for middle management professionals.

BlueSteps
http://www.bluesteps.com
Online global community of senior executives and career-management service that provides executives with exposure to search firms.

ExecuNet
http://www.execunet.com
Membership-based executive referral network.

NETSHARE.com
http://www.netshare.com
Membership-based organization that provides executives with $100K+ job listings and networking opportunities.

RiteSite.com

http://www.ritesite.com

Helps senior executives contact and build relationships with 485 retained executive-search firms.

Executive REGISTRY

www.executiveregistry.com

$100K+ jobs via executive recruiters.

TheLadders

http://TheLadders.com

Online community catering exclusively to the $100K+ job market and offering on-line job-search resources and content for the $100K+ job seekers and recruiters.

TheFENG.org

http://www.thefeng.org

Networking group for financial executives

MENG

http://www.mengonline.com

National network of top-level marketing executives.

CIO.com

http://www.cio.com

Serves chief information officers and other IT leaders and provides technology and business leaders with insight and analysis on information technology trends and an understanding of IT's role in achieving business goals.

LinkedIn

http://LinkedIn.com

Online network of more than 40 million experienced professionals from around the world, representing more than 150 industries.

CEO Express

http://www.ceoexpress.com/default.asp

Business portal for executives.

Boardroom Insider

http://boardroominsider.com

Insights on governance, boards of directors, and the 21st Century boardroom.

InSide Job

http://apps.facebook.com/insidejob

Facebook application to connect candidates with jobs.

RIFProofing

www.rifproofing.com

Three-part, seven-step process specifically designed to help people identify the skills, experiences, and accomplishments that may otherwise go unrecognized.

Candidate's Chair

http://candidateschair.com

Practical guide to job search and networking built from candidate experiences.

Working with recruiters

Quintessential Careers Recruiter/Headhunter Resources, Directories & Associations

http://www.quintcareers.com/recruiter_directories.html

Online Recruiter's Directory

http://www.onlinerecruitersdirectory.com

Online recruiters directory of headhunters, executive search firms, and executive recruiters.

Oya's Directory of Recruiters

http://www.i-recruit.com/about.html

Online directory of links to recruiter Websites.

Salary and compensation research resources

Quintessential Careers Salary Negotiation and Job Offer Tools and Resources for Job-Seekers

www.quintcareers.com/salary_negotiation.html

Collection of job offer, salary information, and salary negotiation resources for job-seekers.

Job Search Intelligence

www.jobsearchintelligence.com

Salary research tool for job-seekers, with a comprehensive set of questions to provide accurate compensation data.

Salary.com

www.Salary.com

On-demand compensation data site that offers Executive Salary Wizard (*http://swz.salary.com/execcomp/layoutscripts/excl_companysearch.asp*) that enables users to enter an executive name, company name, or company ticker symbol below to search a database of executive compensation at publicly held companies.

Salary Expert

www.salaryexpert.com

Offers both free and paid salary reports.

The Salary Calculator

http://us.thesalarycalculator.co.uk

Salary research tool that will also compute real estate values and moving expenses.

Vault

www.vault.com/salaries.jsp

Salary surveys.

JobStar Salary Info

http://jobstar.org/tools/salary/index.php

Highly regarded library-based site that provides links to and descriptions of 300+ free salary surveys.

Background-checking and reference-checking resources

Quintessential Careers Job References Services for Job-Seekers [*http://www.quintcareers.com/job_reference_services.html*], a collection of job history, reference-checking, background-checking, and official transcript services.

Interviewing resources

General interviewing: Carole Martin, The Interview Coach, *http://www.interviewcoach.com.*

Behavioral-interview questions: Complete List of Behavioral Interview Questions, *http://blog.emurse.com/2007/05/21/complete-list-of-behavioral-interview-questions.*

Case interviewing: Quintessential Careers Case Interview Tools and Resources for Job-Seekers, *http://www.quintcareers.com/case_interview_resources.html*, tools and resources for case interviews, in which the candidate is asked to analyze a situation in a short timeframe.

Phone interviewing: Phone Interview Pro, *www.phoneinterviewpro.com*, a fee-based service that simulates an actual phone interview and evaluates users on their performance; site also sells a book, *The Official Phone Interview Handbook.*

Presentation interviews: InterviewBest, *www.interviewbest.com*, fee-based Web-enabled interview strategy that provides candidates with a customized printable presentation to take to the interview.

Books

Executive job search

Job Search Debugged, by Rita Ashley, e-book available from *www.jobsearchdebugged.com/products.asp.*

For Executives Only, by Bill Belnap and Helene Seiler, The Five O'Clock Club, 2007.

Executive Job Search for $100,000 to $1 Million+ Jobs, by Wendy S. Enelow and Louise M. Kursmark, Impact Publications, 2006.

The Executive Job Search, by Orrin Wood, McGraw Hill, 2003.

The Executive Rules: A Complete Guide to Landing an Executive Job, by Thad Greer, Young Author Publications, 2008.

Interviewing

Interview Magic, by Susan Britton Whitcomb, JIST Works, 2005.

Networking

I'm on LinkedIn – Now What???: A Guide to Getting the Most OUT of LinkedIn, Second edition, by Jason Alba, Happy About, 2008.

Salary negotiation

Negotiating Your Salary: How To Make $1,000 A Minute, by Jack Chapman, Ten Speed Press, 2008.

Working with recruiters

Executive Search and Your Career, authored and published by The Association of Executive Search Consultants, 2008.

Headhunters Revealed! Career Secrets for Choosing and Using Professional Recruiters by Darrell W. Gurney, Hunter Arts Publishing, 2000.

The Job Seeker's Guide to Working With Recruiters, authored and published by Kennedy Information, 2009.

Personal branding

Career Distinction: Stand Out by Building Your Brand, by William Arruda and Kirsten Dixson, Wiley, 2007.

Brand Yourself: How to Create an Identity for a Brilliant Career, by David Andrusia and Rick Haskins, Ballantine Books, 2000.

Resumes and cover letters

Top Notch Executive Resumes, by Katharine Hansen, Career Press, 2008.

Professional executive interview coaches

Key to certifications

ACCC: Associate Certified Career Coach

ACC: Associate Certified Coach

CARW: Certified Advanced Resume Writer

CCM: Credentialed Career Manager

CCMC: Certified Career Management Coach

CCS: Certified Career Strategist

CDFI: Career Development Facilitator Instructor

CEC: Certified Executive Coach

CECC: Certified Executive Career Coach

CEIP: Certified Employment Interview Professional

CERW: Certified Expert Resume Writer

CFRWC: Certified Federal Resume Writer

CHRP: Certified Human Resources Professional

CIS: Certified Interview Strategist

CJSS: Certified Job Search Strategist

CLTMC: Certified Leadership and Talent Management Coach

CMPBS: Certified Master Personal Branding Strategist

CMF: Career Management Fellow

COIMS: Certified Online Identity Management Strategist

COIS: Certified Online Identity Strategist

CPBS: Certified Personal Branding Strategist

CPRC: Certified Professional Retirement Coach

CPS: Certified Professional Secretary

CPRW: Certified Professional Resume Writer

CPRWCC: Certified Professional Resume Writer and Career Coach

CRS: Certified Resume Strategist

CTL: Certified Teleclass Leader

CTMS: Certified Transition Management Seminars

CTSB: Certified Targeted Small Business, State of Iowa

DCC: Distance Career Counselor

DCF: Distance Credentialed Facilitator

FJSTC: Federal Job Search Trainer and Coach

GCDF: Global Career Development Facilitator

GCDFI: Global Career Development Facilitator Instructor

IJCTC/JCTC: [International] Job and Career Transition Coach

LEA: Licensed Employment Agent

MCC: Master Career Counselor

MCCC: Master Certified Career Coach

MCDP: Master Career Development Professional

MRW: Master Resume Writer

NCC: National Board Certified Counselor

NCCC: National Board Certified Career Counselor

NCRW: Nationally Certified Resume Writer

PHR: Professional in Human Resources

Interview coaches who coach executives exclusively

Rita Ashley
Job Search Coach
4636 Cloudcrest Dr.
Medford, OR 97504
rfa@ritaashley.com
http://jobsearchdebugged.com

Louise Kursmark, MRW, CCM, CEIP, JCTC
Best Impression Career Services
24 White Oaks Lane, Reading, MA 01867
781-944-2471
LK@yourbestimpression.com
www.yourbestimpression.com

Cindy Kraft, CPBS, CCMC, CCM, JCTC
Executive Essentials
P.O. Box 336
Valrico, FL 33595
813-655-0658
cindy@cfo-coach.com
www.cfo-coach.com

Don Orlando, MBA, CPRW, JCTC, CCM, CCMC, CJSS
The McLean Group
640 South McDonough Street
Montgomery, AL 36104
334-264-2020
yourcareercoach@charterinternet.com
www.linkedin.com/in/donorlandocareercoach

Ford R. Myers, CEC
Career Potential, LLC
250 W. Montgomery Avenue, Suite J
Haverford, PA 19041
888-967-5762 or 610-649-1778
contact@careerpotential.com
www.careerpotential.com

Beverly Harvey, CCMC, CCM, CLMTC, JCTC
HarveyCareers
PO Box 750
Pierson, FL 32180
386-749-3111
beverly@harveycareers.com
www.harveycareers.com

Judy Rosemarin, MA
Sense-Able Strategies, Inc.
170 West Broadway Suite 8A
Long Beach, NY 11561
212-946-4986
Judy@sense-ablestrategies.com
www.sense-ablestrategies.com

Interview coaches who specialize in coaching executives

Meg Montford, MCCC, CMF
Abilities Enhanced
PO Box 11823
Kansas City, MO 64138
816-767-1196
meg@abilitiesenhanced.com
www.abilitiesenhanced.com

Barb Poole, CCMC, CLTMC, PHR
Hire Imaging, LLC
1812 Red Fox Road
St. Cloud, MN 56301
320-253-0975 or 877-265-2750
barb@hireimaging.com
www.hireimaging.com

Cheryl Palmer, CECC, CPRW
Call to Career
P.O. Box 4665
Silver Spring, MD 20914
301-642-8076
admin@calltocareer.com
www.calltocareer.com

Don Goodman, CPRW, CCMC, CJSS
800-909-0109
dgoodman@GotTheJob.com
www.GotTheJob.com

Fred Coon, LEA, JCTC, CRW
Stewart, Cooper & Coon, Inc.
2111 E. Highland Ave. Ste. B-190
Phoenix, AZ 85016
602-385-3000; ext. 200
www.stewartcoopercoon.com

Randy Block, CCMC, CPRC, IJCTC
PO Box 1047
Boyes Hot Springs, CA 95416
415-383-6471
randy@randyblock.com
www.randyblock.com

Laura M. Labovich, CCM, CARW, Master of Labor Relations and Human Resources, Five O'Clock Club Certified Coach, 360Reach Certified Analyst
Aspire! Empower!
8910 Seneca Lane
Bethesda, MD 20817
703-942-9390
aspireempower@gmail.com
www.aspire-empower.com

Donna Beestman
Career Success Strategies, LLC
9 Southwick Circle
Madison, WI 53717
608-831-5226
donna.beestman@tds.net
www.CareerSuccessStrategies.com

Robyn Feldberg, CCMC, NCRW, CJSS
Abundant Success Career Services
11732 Humberside Drive, Frisco, TX 75035
972-464-1144; 866-WIN-AJOB
Robyn@AbundantSuccessCoach.com
AbundantSuccessCoach.com

Divya Gupta, MBA, ACCC, CPRW
Confident Career Corporation
Naperville, IL 60540
630-364-1848
divya@confidentcareer.com
www.confidentcareer.com

Susan Guarneri, NCCC, CCMC, CEIP, DCC, MCC, CERW, CMPBS, COIMS
Guarneri Associates
6670 Crystal Lake Road
Three Lakes, WI 54562
866-881-4055
Susan@AssessmentGoddess.com
www.AssessmentGoddess.com
www.Resume-Magic.com

Annemarie Cross, CEIP, Certified Reach Online Identity Strategist, Certified Reach Personal Branding Strategist
Advanced Employment Concepts
PO Box 91, Hallam Victoria 3803 Australia
+613 9708 6930
info@a-e-c.com.au
www.a-e-c.com.au

Georgia Adamson, JCTC, CEIP
A Successful Career
1096 N. Central Ave.
San Jose, CA 95128
408-244-6402
coach@asuccessfulcareer.com
www.ablueribbonresume.com
www.asuccessfulcareer.com

Sharon McCormick, MCC, NCCC, NCC, Qualified Myers-Briggs Test Administrator
Sharon McCormick Expert Career & HR Consulting
4711 Hope Valley Road
Durham, NC 27707
919-424-1244
careertreasure@gmail.com
www.careertreasure.com

Lauren Milligan
ResuMAYDAY
29W678 Stevens Ct.
Warrenville, IL 60555
630-836-9910 or 888-556-2776
lauren@resumayday.com
www.ResuMAYDAY.com

Elene Cafasso, MBA, ACC, Coaches Training Institute-trained
Enerpace, Inc. Executive Coaching
240 N. Addison
Elmhurst, IL 60126
630-832-4399
mail@enerpace.com
www.enerpace.com

Interview coaches whose practices include executives

Judit E. Price, MS, CCM, CPRW, IJCTC, CDFI
Berke and Price, Skills for Career Success
6 Newtowne Way
Chelmsford, MA 01824
978-256-0482; Mobile: 978-764-7238
jprice@careercampaign.com
www.careercampaign.com

Joan Runnheim Olson, CLTMC, CCMC, ACC, Certified Five O'Clock Club
Career Coach
Pathways Career Success Strategies
1901 Hawthorne Pointe
Hudson, WI 54016
715-808-0344
joan@pathwayscareer.com
www.pathwayscareer.com

Billie R. Sucher, MS, CTMS, CTSB, JCTC, CCM
Billie Sucher Career Transition Services
7177 Hickman Road, Suite 10
Urbandale, IA 50322
515-276-0061
billie@billiesucher.com
www.billiesucher.com

Jane Finkle, MS, NCC, MCDP
Career Visions
1601 Walnut Street, Suite 1408
Philadelphia, PA 19102
215-564-5277
info@careervisions.cc
www.careervisions.cc

Elizabeth Craig, MBA, MCDP, CCM, GCDF, GCDFI, DCF, Internationally
Certified Career and Job Search Strategist, Life Purpose Coach
ELC (Energize. Leverage. Connect.) Global, LLC
P.O. Box 46271
Eden Prairie, MN 55344-2971
952-944-1759
561-627-0490
elizabeth@elcglobal.com
http://www.elcglobal.com

Bettina Seidman
SEIDBET Associates
PO Box 147
Madison Square Station
New York, NY 10159
212-260-2026
SEIDBET@aol.com
www.seidbet.com

Index